Francisco Pizarro

and the Conquest of the Inca

Explorers of New Lands

Explorers of New Lands

Francisco Pizarro
and the Conquest of the Inca

Shane Mountjoy

Series Consulting Editor William H. Goetzmann
Jack S. Blanton, Sr. Chair in History and American Studies
University of Texas, Austin

CHELSEA HOUSE
PUBLISHERS
A Haights Cross Communications ✦ Company ®
Philadelphia

COVER: A portrait of Francisco Pizarro

CHELSEA HOUSE PUBLISHERS
VP, NEW PRODUCT DEVELOPMENT Sally Cheney
DIRECTOR OF PRODUCTION Kim Shinners
CREATIVE MANAGER Takeshi Takahashi
MANUFACTURING MANAGER Diann Grasse

Staff for FRANCISCO PIZARRO
EXECUTIVE EDITOR Lee Marcott
EDITORIAL ASSISTANT Carla Greenberg
PRODUCTION EDITOR Noelle Nardone
PHOTO EDITOR Sarah Bloom
COVER AND INTERIOR DESIGNER Keith Trego
LAYOUT 21st Century Publishing and Communications, Inc.

© 2006 by Chelsea House Publishers,
a subsidiary of Haights Cross Communications.

A Haights Cross Communications Company ®

www.chelseahouse.com

First Printing

9 8 7 6 5 4 3 2 1

Library of Congress Cataloging-in-Publication Data

Mountjoy, Shane, 1967–
    Francisco Pizarro and the conquest of the Inca/Shane Mountjoy.
        p. cm.–(Explorers of new lands)
    Includes bibliographical references and index.
    ISBN 0-7910-8614-3 (hardcover)
  1. Pizarro, Francisco, ca. 1475–1541–Juvenile literature. 2. Peru–History–Conquest,
1522–1548–Juvenile literature. 3. Incas–Juvenile literature. 4. Explorers–Peru–Biography–
Juvenile literature. 5. Explorers–Spain–Biography–Juvenile literature. I. Title. II. Series
    F3442.P6725M68 2005
    985'.02'092–dc22
                                                                        2005007519

Table of Contents

Introduction

by William H. Goetzmann
Jack S. Blanton, Sr. Chair in History and American Studies
University of Texas, Austin

Explorers have always been adventurers. They were, and still are, people of vision and most of all, people of curiosity. The English poet Rudyard Kipling once described the psychology behind the explorer's curiosity:

"Something hidden. Go and find it. Go and
   look behind the Ranges—
Something lost behind the Ranges. Lost and
   waiting for you. Go!" [1]

Miguel de Cervantes, the heroic author of *Don
Quixote*, longed to be an explorer-conquistador. So
he wrote a personal letter to King Phillip II of
Spain asking to be appointed to lead an expedition
to the New World. Phillip II turned down his
request. Later, while in prison, Cervantes gained
revenge. He wrote the immortal story of *Don
Quixote*, a broken-down, half-crazy "Knight of La
Mancha" who "explored" Spain with his faithful
sidekick, Sancho Panza. His was perhaps the first
of a long line of revenge novels—a lampoon of the
real explorer-conquistadors.

Most of these explorer-conquistadors, such as
Columbus and Cortés, are often regarded as heroes
who discovered new worlds and empires. They
were courageous, brave and clever, but most of
them were also cruel to the native peoples they
met. For example, Cortés, with a small band of
500 Spanish conquistadors, wiped out the vast

Aztec Empire. He insulted the Aztecs' gods and tore down their temples. A bit later, far down in South America, Francisco Pizarro and Hernando de Soto did the same to the Inca Empire, which was hidden behind a vast upland desert among Peru's towering mountains. Both tasks seem to be impossible, but these conquistadors not only overcame nature and savage armies, they stole their gold and became rich nobles. More astounding, they converted whole countries and even a continent to Spanish Catholicism. Cathedrals replaced blood-soaked temples, and the people of South and Central America, north to the Mexican border, soon spoke only two languages—Portuguese in Brazil and Spanish in the rest of the countries, even extending through the Southwest United States.

Most of the cathedral building and language changing has been attributed to the vast numbers of Spanish and Portuguese missionaries, but trade with and even enslavement of the natives must have played a great part. Also playing an important part were great missions that were half churches and half farming and ranching communities. They offered protection from enemies and a life of stability for the natives. Clearly vast numbers of natives took to these missions. The missions vied with the cruel native caciques, or rulers, for protection and for a constant food supply. We have to ask ourselves: Did the Spanish conquests raise the natives' standard of living? And did a religion of love appeal more to the natives than ones of sheer terror, where hearts were torn out and bodies were tossed down steep temple stairways as sacrifices that were probably eaten by dogs or other wild beasts? These questions are something to think about as you read the Explorers of New Lands series. They are profound questions even today.

"New Lands" does not only refer to the Western Hemisphere and the Spanish/Portuguese conquests there. Our series should probably begin with the fierce Vikings—Eric the Red, who discovered Greenland in 982, and Leif Ericson, who discovered North America in 1002, followed, probably a year later, by a settler named Bjorni. The Viking sagas (or tales passed down through generations) tell the stories of these men and of Fredis, the first woman discoverer of a New Land. She became a savior of the Viking men when, wielding a broadsword and screaming like a madwoman, she single-handedly routed the native Beothuks who were about to wipe out the earliest Viking settlement in North America that can be identified. The Vikings did not, however, last as long in North America as they did in Greenland and Northern England. The natives of the north were far tougher than the natives of the south and the Caribbean.

Far away, on virtually the other side of the world, traders were making their way east toward China. Persians and Arabs as well as Mongols established a trade route to the Far East via such fabled cities as Samarkand, Bukhara, and Kashgar and across the Hindu Kush and Pamir Mountains to Tibet and beyond. One of our volumes tells the story of Marco Polo, who crossed from Byzantium (later Constantinople) overland along the Silk Road to China and the court of Kublai Khan, the Mongol emperor. This was a crossing over wild deserts and towering mountains, as long as Columbus's Atlantic crossing to the Caribbean. His journey came under less dangerous (no pirates yet) and more comfortable conditions than that of the Polos, Nicolo and Maffeo, who from 1260 to 1269 made their way across these endless wastes while making friends, not enemies, of the fierce Mongols. In 1271, they took along Marco Polo (who was Nicolo's son and Maffeo's nephew). Marco became a great favorite of Kublai Khan and stayed in China till 1292. He even became the ruler of one of Kublai Khan's largest cities, Hangchow.

Before he returned, Marco Polo had learned of many of the Chinese ports, and because of Chinese trade to the west across the Indian Ocean, he knew of East Africa as far as Zanzibar. He also knew of the Spice Islands and Japan. When he returned to his home city of Venice he brought enviable new knowledge with him, about gunpowder, paper and paper money, coal, tea making, and the role of worms that create silk! While captured by Genoese forces, he dictated an account of his amazing adventures, which included vast amounts of new information, not only about China, but about the geography of nearly half of the globe. This is one hallmark of great explorers. How much did they contribute to the world's body of knowledge? These earlier inquisitive explorers were important members of a culture of science that stemmed from world trade and genuine curiosity. For the Polos, crossing over deserts, mountains and very dangerous tribal-dominated countries or regions, theirs was a hard-won knowledge. As you read about Marco Polo's travels, try and count the many new things and descriptions he brought to Mediterranean countries.

Besides the Polos, however, there were many Islamic traders who traveled to China, like Ibn Battuta, who came from Morocco in Northwest Africa. An Italian Jewish rabbi-trader, Jacob d'Ancona, made his way via India in 1270 to the great Chinese trading port of Zaitun, where he spent much of his time. Both of these explorer-travelers left extensive reports of their expeditions, which rivaled those of the Polos but were less known, as are the neglected accounts of Roman Catholic friars who entered China, one of whom became bishop of Zaitun.[2]

In 1453, the Turkish Empire cut off the Silk Road to Asia. But Turkey was thwarted when, in 1497 and 1498, the Portuguese captain Vasco da Gama sailed from Lisbon around the tip of Africa, up to Arab-controlled Mozambique, and across the

Indian Ocean to Calicut on the western coast of India. He faced the hostility of Arab traders who virtually dominated Calicut. He took care of this problem on a second voyage in 1502 with 20 ships to safeguard the interests of colonists brought to India by another Portuguese captain, Pedro Álvares Cabral. Da Gama laid siege to Calicut and destroyed a fleet of 29 warships. He secured Calicut for the Portuguese settlers and opened a spice route to the islands of the Indies that made Portugal and Spain rich. Spices were valued nearly as much as gold since without refrigeration, foods would spoil. The spices disguised this, and also made the food taste good. Virtually every culture in the world has some kind of stew. Almost all of them depend on spices. Can you name some spices that come from the faraway Spice Islands?

Of course most Americans have heard of Christopher Columbus, who in 1492 sailed west across the Atlantic for the Indies and China. Instead, on four voyages, he reached Hispaniola (now Haiti and the Dominican Republic), Cuba and Jamaica. He created a vision of a New World, populated by what he misleadingly called Indians.

Conquistadors like the Italian sailing for Portugal, Amerigo Vespucci, followed Columbus and in 1502 reached South America at what is now Brazil. His landing there explains Brazil's Portuguese language origins as well as how America got its name on Renaissance charts drawn on vellum or dried sheepskin.

Meanwhile, the English heard of a Portuguese discovery of marvelous fishing grounds off Labrador (discovered by the Vikings and rediscovered by a mysterious freelance Portuguese sailor named the "Labrador"). They sent John Cabot in 1497 to locate these fishing grounds. He found them, and Newfoundland and Labrador as well. It marked the British discovery of North America.

In this first series there are strange tales of other explorers of new lands—Juan Ponce de León, who sought riches and possibly a fountain of youth (everlasting life) and died in Florida; Francisco Coronado, whose men discovered the Grand Canyon and at Zuñi established what became the heart of the Spanish Southwest before the creation of Santa Fe; and de Soto, who after helping to conquer the Incas, boldly ravaged what is now the

American South and Southeast. He also found that the Indian Mound Builder cultures, centered in Cahokia across the Mississippi from present-day St. Louis, had no gold and did not welcome him. Garcilaso de la Vega, the last Inca, lived to write de Soto's story, called *The Florida of the Inca*—a revenge story to match that of Cervantes, who like Garcilaso de la Vega ended up in the tiny Spanish town of Burgos. The two writers never met. Why was this—especially since Cervantes was the tax collector? Perhaps this was when he was in prison writing *Don Quixote*.

In 1513 Vasco Núñez de Balboa discovered the Pacific Ocean "from a peak in Darien"[3] and was soon beheaded by a rival conquistador. But perhaps the greatest Pacific feat was Ferdinand Magellan's voyage around the world from 1519 to 1522, which he did not survive.

Magellan was a Portuguese who sailed for Spain down the Atlantic and through the Strait of Magellan—a narrow passage to the Pacific. He journeyed across that ocean to the Philippines, where he was killed in a fight with the natives. As a recent biography put it, he had "sailed over the edge of the world."[4] His men continued west, and the *Victoria,* the last of his five ships, worn and battered, reached Spain.

Sir Francis Drake, a privateer and lifelong enemy of Spain, sailed for Queen Elizabeth of England on a secret mission in 1577 to find a passage across the Americas for England. Though he sailed, as he put it, "along the backside of Nueva Espanola"[5] as far north as Alaska perhaps, he found no such passage. He then sailed west around the world to England. He survived to help defeat the huge Spanish Armada sent by Phillip II to take England in 1588. Alas he could not give up his bad habit of privateering, and died of dysentery off Porto Bello, Panama. Drake did not find what he was looking for "beyond the ranges," but it wasn't his curiosity that killed him. He may have been the greatest explorer of them all!

While reading our series of great explorers, think about the many questions that arise in your reading, which I hope inspires you to great deeds.

Notes

1. Rudyard Kipling, "The Explorer" (1898). See Jon Heurtl, *Rudyard Kipling: Selected Poems* (New York: Barnes & Noble Books, 2004), 7.

2. Jacob D'Ancona, David Shelbourne, translator, *The City of Light: The Hidden Journal of the Man Who Entered China Four Years Before Marco Polo* (New York: Citadel Press, 1997).

3. John Keats, "On First Looking Into Chapman's Homer."

4. Laurence Bergreen, *Over the Edge of the World: Magellan's Terrifying Circumnavigation of the Globe* (New York: William Morrow & Company, 2003).

5. See Richard Hakluyt, *Principal Navigations, Voyages, Traffiques and Discoveries of the English Nation*; section on Sir Francis Drake.

An Important Choice

It was November 15, 1532. A group of about 180 Spaniards stood at the edge of a high mountain in western South America. In the valley below was an army of 50,000 Indians. The Incan warriors filled much of the area on the far side of the city in the valley, as well as the mountainside across from the Spaniards. The Spaniards thought the vast Incan camp had so many men that it was "nothing else than a very starry sky."[1] One of them said that "it filled us all with amazement."[2] The Spanish leader was a tall, aging man. His name was Francisco Pizarro. All his life he had dreamed of winning riches and land on the field of battle. Now that opportunity lay before him and his men.

Pizarro watched the large Incan camp in the valley below. He had dreamed of such an opportunity for years. In two earlier expeditions, he had failed to come so close. He and his men had faced starvation. Hostile Indians using poison-tipped arrows had killed some of his men. They had even come across cannibals. Both expeditions had suffered from a lack of adequate supplies and financing. To many, it certainly seemed that the man in his 50s had missed his chance for greatness.

But Francisco Pizarro was not someone who easily gave up. Despite all the hardships and failures, he continued to believe that gold and silver were waiting for the Spaniards in the land of the Inca. He had seen jewelry and other items made of the precious metals. For several years now, Pizarro was convinced that the stories of great wealth in the land of the Inca were true. Now he was very near the emperor and his army. Soon, he would see for himself if the Inca possessed gold and silver.

Pizarro and his men first struck out into Incan territory about seven months earlier. As they traveled to the interior, Indians welcomed them with gifts and food. They also passed many Incan forts. The forts were deserted. Most of them were easily defensible against his force. But the Incan emperor allowed his small force to pass through Incan territory untouched. Some might call it luck. Others might think the emperor was foolish. But Pizarro believed that any success depended on his faith in God and his boldness.

A DARING PLAN

Pizarro had an idea of what he wanted to do. It was simple, but it was also bold. Rather than focus on defeating the emperor's army, he intended to capture the emperor. His relative Hernándo Cortés conquered the Aztecs by seizing their emperor. Pizarro hoped for similar success against the Inca. However, Pizarro did not know what he might do after capturing the emperor.

Francisco Pizarro leads his men through the Andes Mountains on the way to meet the Inca at Cajamarca. There, Pizarro and his 180 soldiers came upon a vast army of 50,000 Indians.

Pizarro's attention again turned to the Incas in the valley. How could such a small group of men even hope to survive the great army waiting for them? How could they hope to win their long sought-after victory over the Incas? How could they capture the emperor when such a large force protected him? Pizarro thought back to the training he received as a teenager—training that did not accept retreat. Pizarro knew that danger awaited them in the valley. But the valley also offered the chance for greatness. He had worked for many years for this opportunity. The cost to this point had been great: failed voyages, dangerous expeditions, and broken friendships. Now he stared at the Incan army sprawled across the valley. His men were quite aware of the size of the army waiting for them. One of his soldiers later wrote that the sight of the Indian camp "caused something like confusion and even fear."[3] He looked at his men and saw the fear in their eyes.

Pizarro had faced fear before. Trained as a soldier, he had overcome his fears in the past by advancing forward. In battle, he believed in attacking rather than waiting for his enemy to attack him.

But the Incan army was so large. There were so many tents, so many warriors waiting for them. Pizarro studied the situation as the unit guarding their rear caught up to them. He knew that one of two things waited for them in the valley: either death or greatness. He knew that either his force would win a great victory over the Incas or they would die trying. He looked at the Incan army one more time. It was a magnificent sight. He could see thousands of tents and warriors, and all the activity that takes place in a large camp. Equally impressive, the camp operated in a calm and orderly fashion. Pizarro weighed his options before deciding what to do. He made up his mind, and then never looked back. Despite the dangers and fears, Pizarro believed, as did one of his soldiers, that "it was too late to turn back . . . "[4] He gave the order to proceed down into the valley. Pizarro chose to risk death to achieve greatness. Like many other times in his life, Pizarro chose boldness.

By the end of the next day, Pizarro's boldness helped him to capture the Incan emperor. On that one day, the Spaniards won a battle that all but guaranteed them control of the Incan Empire. But the story of Pizarro's great victory started nearly 60 years earlier. And it all began with the birth of a poor boy to a humble family in Europe. That boy grew up and changed the Incan world forever. That boy became a conquistador. That boy was Francisco Pizarro—conqueror of the Incas.

Test Your Knowledge

1 How many Incas awaited Pizarro and his men in the valley below?

a. 5,000

b. A force equal to Pizarro's

c. A force five times that of Pizarro's

d. 50,000

2 What did Pizarro believe the Spaniards could gain from the Incas?

a. The secret to eternal youth

b. Rare native medicines unheard of in Europe

c. Gold and silver

d. Diamonds

3 How had Pizarro and his men crossed so far into Incan territory?

a. They had defeated every Inca force that had confronted them.

b. The emperor of the Incas had let them pass.

c. They had bribed local Inca tribal leaders.

d. None of the above.

4 How did Pizarro plan to defeat the much larger Incan force?

a. By capturing the Inca emperor

b. With poison-tipped arrows

c. By frightening the Incas with musket fire

d. With cannons

5 To what other great Spanish explorer and leader
was Pizarro related?
a. Francisco Coronado
b. Juan Ponce de León
c. Hernándo Cortés
d. None of the above

ANSWERS: 1. d; 2. c; 3. b; 4. a; 5. c

Pizarro and
His World

THE YOUNG CONQUISTADOR

Francisco Pizarro was born in the city of Trujillo, Spain. Trujillo was in the province of Estremadura in southwestern Spain. Pizarro was born sometime in the 1470s, probably in 1475. Historians are not sure of the exact date or year.

Pizarro's province of Estremadura produced many future conquistadors for Spain. Estremadura's climate and terrain help explain this. During the summer, the region is hot and dry. During the winter, the region endures freezing temperatures and harsh conditions. The name Estremadura itself comes from the Latin *extrema et dura*, which means "remote and hard." People in Estremadura lived in a remote and hard land, and this hard and remote region formed ruthless conquerors like Hernándo Cortés, Vasco Núñez de Balboa, Pedro de Alvarado, Pedro de Valdivia, and Francisco Pizarro. Also, many of the men who helped Cortés and Pizarro conquer great empires came from the province of Estremadura.

Francisco was the son of a Spanish gentleman, Gonzalo Pizarro.[5] Gonzalo was a colonel in the Spanish Army and fought in many battles. Some called his father "the Tall," which drew attention to his height. Others knew him as the "One-Eyed," since he lost an eye in one of his many military battles. Francisco's mother was a woman named Francisca González.[6] His mother and father never married each other. Thus, Francisco was an

A statue of Francisco Pizarro stands in his birthplace of Trujillo, Spain, which is in the province of Estremadura. Many future conquistadors, like Hernándo Cortés and Vasco Núñez de Balboa, were also born in the province.

illegitimate child. This meant he had no legal right to inherit his father's property or title. Gonzalo Pizarro had other sons: Hernando, Gonzalo, and Juan. Of these three, only Hernando was a legal heir. Each of his brothers later played important roles in Francisco's conquest of the Inca.

Without legal rights to either a title or property, Francisco Pizarro faced many difficulties in improving his status. During this time, few options were available to someone who lacked a title or property. The only ways to improve one's status were to marry into nobility, achieve some great victory in the military, or gain recognition as legitimate by the king. By marrying into a noble family, one could gain noble status. Often, to reward a *conquistador*, or conqueror, monarchs might grant such soldiers a title of nobility. Lastly, one could ask the king to declare his child legitimate. Each of these options provided opportunities for illegitimate children to gain the full rights of inheritance. Pizarro chose to improve his status through military success.

PIZARRO'S CHILDHOOD

Historians know little about Pizarro's early years.

There are several stories about his childhood.
One says that his mother left him on the steps of
a church. Another tale claims that he lived with
pigs and even nursed on a pig, which seems
unlikely.[7] A more believable story tells how his
grandparents raised him. Most historians think
that he grew up in the care of his mother's parents.
His opportunities were limited. He grew up without attending school. He never learned to read
or write. Even as an adult, Pizarro was illiterate.
As a young boy, he spent most of his time working as a swineherd—that is, he took care of pigs.
Although such work might seem unpleasant, it
was a good job for a commoner.

Francisco Pizarro grew restless with his life in
Spain. He seemed unwilling to accept his rank in
Spanish society. Life in Spain offered Pizarro
poverty and obscurity. Life in Spain offered a rela-
tively safe existence. But Pizarro did not want to
live out his life in poverty. He chose to leave his
hometown to try to earn a higher position in life.
Like his father before him, he became a soldier in
the Spanish Army. He probably began fighting in
the late 1490s.

Francisco fought for the Spanish against the French. At the time, the two countries waged war against each other in Italy. It was in Italy that he learned a great deal about warfare, fighting, and leading a fighting force. In Italy, he learned to fight boldly, even when facing overwhelming odds. He learned to treat his enemies with cruelty. From these war experiences, he discovered that the path to greatness for him came in winning battles and conquering other people. When Pizarro came to the New World, he already had the training and skills necessary to conquer the Incas. But he would wait 30 years before achieving his dreams for greatness.

THE UNIFICATION OF SPAIN

When Pizarro was born, war raged on the Iberian Peninsula, the landmass in southwestern Europe. Today, Spain and Portugal occupy the entire peninsula. (The Iberian Peninsula gets its name from the ancient Greeks, who called its residents Iberians. Those ancient people and the peninsula probably got their name from the peninsula's second-longest river, the Ebro, or Iberus.) Beginning in the early 700s, a group of people invaded the Iberian Peninsula from Northern Africa. These invaders were the Moors. The Moors were Arab Muslims who extended their territory into Europe. They crossed the Mediterranean Sea near Gibraltar and captured most of the Iberian Peninsula by 718. The Moors never managed to drive all of the Christian kingdoms from the Iberian Peninsula. For nearly four centuries, the mountainous region in northern Spain was all that remained free of Moorish control.

The Moors made Córdoba their capital city. Córdoba was on an important river (the Guadalquivir) in southern Spain. While the Moors ruled, Spain enjoyed growth in architecture, the arts, and literature. The Moors built mosques (Muslim places of worship) and castles (called *alcazars*). They also preserved many ancient Greek and Latin writings, as well as writings from the Middle East. European scholars traveled to Spain to study these ancient works. The Moors allowed Christians and Jews to live in their society. Many of these non-Moorish peoples helped contribute to the flourishing Moorish culture.

As their culture prospered, the strength of the Moorish military weakened. The central government grew weak. Smaller, independent Moorish states and cities no longer supported the central government. Since the Moors first conquered Spain, they allowed some of the Christian kingdoms to continue ruling at the local level. As the central government weakened, these Christian kingdoms grew tired of Moorish rule.

Over time, the remaining Christian kingdoms grew stronger. They began to fight the Moors and reclaim parts of Spain. First, they were only in northern Spain. Then, the Christian kingdoms expanded their holdings to include much of the land in northern Spain stretching from the Atlantic Ocean to the Mediterranean Sea. Eventually, the Christian kingdoms pushed the Moors farther and farther to the south. Castile, a Christian kingdom in north-central Spain, became the strongest non-Moorish kingdom. Castile led the fight to push the Moors off the peninsula.

But Castile did not always get its way. Beginning in the 1100s, a group in western Spain won its independence from Castile. This area later became Portugal. By about 1250, the Portuguese controlled all of their present-day territory.

During the 1100s, to strengthen themselves, the Christian kingdoms began meeting together in a parliament, called a *Cortes*. Representatives from the Catholic Church, the nobility, and even the middle class met in the Cortes. The Cortes increased support for the war effort among the people, but the Spanish kings still held most of the power in their kingdoms.

The Christian kingdoms continued to defeat the Moors. Finally, by the late 1200s, only the Kingdom of Granada remained under Moorish control. The Moors struggled to keep their little kingdom independent from Christian rule. But this became more difficult because the Spanish kingdoms kept combining. By 1300, only three kingdoms controlled all of the non-Moorish parts of Spain. These were the Christian kingdoms of Aragon, Castile, and Navarre. Castile was the largest and most powerful of the kingdoms and controlled most of Spain. Aragon ruled most of eastern Spain and the Balearic Islands in the Mediterranean Sea. Navarre, near the mountains in northern Spain, was the smallest of the kingdoms.

Then, two of the kingdoms combined to grow even stronger. In 1469, Ferdinand of Aragon

The marriage of Ferdinand of Aragon and Isabella of Castile, in 1469, united the most powerful of the Spanish kingdoms. Under their leadership, the Spanish fought to force the remaining Moors off the Iberian Peninsula for good.

and Isabella of Castile married each other. Their marriage united the largest and most powerful of the Spanish kingdoms. By 1479, King Ferdinand and Queen Isabella were the ruling monarchs of their combined territories. Nearly all of Christian Spain was now unified and ready to claim the rest of the Iberian Peninsula. Castile conquered the small

(continued on page 22)

Spain and Portugal Divide the World

In 1493, Christopher Columbus returned to Spain from his first voyage to the New World and reported to Ferdinand and Isabella. He was given a large reception. There was great anticipation over his discovery and possible wealth. Columbus presented the little he could: several gold trinkets and a few Indians who survived the voyage. Ferdinand and Isabella were impressed with the possibilities and took steps to protect Columbus's discovery. Spain asked Pope Alexander VI to recognize its control over the lands Columbus had visited. Spain also expressed its desire to take Christianity to the natives there. Since Portugal already claimed extensive areas, both sides argued that they deserved control of the new lands. The pope prevented a possible war between the two Catholic countries by negotiating a compromise. Representatives of Portugal, Spain, and the pope met in the Spanish city of Tordesillas.

In 1494, Portugal and Spain signed an agreement, known as the Treaty of Tordesillas. This agreement basically divided the world between the two countries. Portugal believed Spain's discovery threatened its claims. Spain argued that its discovery was a new route to the Far East or maybe even islands no one knew about before. The Treaty of Tordesillas drew specific lines that separated the Portuguese claims from the Spanish claims. The two European powers agreed that Spain held all claims 370 leagues west of the Portuguese-controlled Cape Verde Islands off the coast of Africa. This line placed Spanish claims over 1,100 nautical miles west of the Cape Verde Islands. This agreement greatly extended Portuguese claims. Previously, the line was about 100 leagues west of the Cape Verde Islands (300 nautical miles).

The Treaty of Tordesillas had two significant results. First, the agreement ended the possibility of war between the countries. Spain benefited from this as it explored and claimed large parts of Central and South America over the next 50 years. Second, the treaty influenced which countries held sway in the New World, especially South America. Since eastern South America fell under Portuguese control, they later established the colony of Brazil. The rest of South and Central America fell under Spanish control. Thus, Portuguese is the main language in Brazil while people in the rest of South and Central America primarily speak Spanish.

(continued from page 19)

kingdom of Navarre in 1512. This conquest joined all of Spain under a single ruler.

After Ferdinand and Isabella united most of Spain, the Spanish decided to push the remaining Moors in Granada off the peninsula. Under the leadership of the combined Aragon and Castile forces, the Moors were finally defeated in January 1492. To strengthen their hold on Spain, Ferdinand and Isabella expelled any Jews who refused to convert to Christianity. And 1492 was also the year of a great discovery.

Test Your Knowledge

1 What does the Latin phrase *"extrema et dura"* mean?
   a. Far and wide
   b. Desolate and hot
   c. Remote and hard
   d. Extremely dry

2 How could an illegitimate child in fifteenth-century Spain improve his status?
   a. The father could petition the king to declare the child legitimate.
   b. The child could grow up and marry into a noble family.
   c. The child could grow up, become a conquistador, and earn a noble title.
   d. All of the above.

3 Who were the Moors?
   a. French soldiers known for their fierceness, but defeated by the Spanish
   b. Arab Muslims who invaded the Iberian Peninsula
   c. North African traders and merchants
   d. An elite group of Spanish conquistadors

4   Which of the following groups were represented in the Christian parliament known as the *Cortes*?

a. The Catholic Church

b. Spanish nobility

c. The middle class

d. All of the above

5   In what year did the Moors suffer their final defeat on the Iberian Peninsula?

a. 1492

b. 1500

c. 1495

d. 1520

ANSWERS: 1. c; 2. d; 3. b; 4. d; 5. a

Spain in the New World

THE NEW WORLD

Of course, besides defeating the Moors in 1492, something else important was happening in Spain that year. That was the year Christopher Columbus sailed to the New World. Columbus was born in Genoa, Italy, but he sailed for the Spanish when he discovered the West Indies. Spain under Ferdinand and Isabella followed Portugal's example in creating trading posts and colonies outside of Europe. European countries wanted to trade with the Far East. Tea, spices, and other goods that Europeans wanted came from the East Indies. Since there was no easy way to trade with the Far East, Portugal began exploring for other ways to travel to and from India and the East Indies. Prince Henry the Navigator of Portugal encouraged his country to explore parts of western Africa. Their travels resulted in trade with African natives. This trade included gold, ivory, and slaves, and helped make Portugal a wealthy nation. Despite Portugal's small size, its explorers later sailed all the way around the southern tip of South Africa.

Christopher Columbus, like the Portuguese, wanted to find a trade route to the East Indies. He and most geographers of his day believed the world was round, and Columbus decided to sail west to get to the East Indies. He also mistakenly believed that the world was much smaller than it is. So instead of reaching Asia, he ended up landing on a group of islands in the Caribbean Sea. Believing

How American Natives Became Known as Indians

When Christopher Columbus landed at San Salvador in 1492, he believed he had arrived in the Far East. The natives who greeted him did not look like Asians, but they did have darker skin than Europeans. Columbus realized he was on an island, but he thought he was in the East Indies. The East Indies are a group of islands near the coast of Asia. Since he was mistaken about where he was, Columbus wrongly named the natives *Indians*. The natives were not Indian since they lived near North America.

Within roughly 30 years, most Europeans recognized that the islands and nearby continent were not part of Asia. This meant that the natives could not be Indians. Europeans realized their mistake. The name stuck, however, and most Europeans continued to call the people of the Americas Indians. Even today, many refer to the native people in the Americas as American Indians. Others prefer Native American.

he had found the East Indies, Columbus claimed the lands for Spain and called the people he found there *Indians.*

SPAIN BECOMES MORE MILITARY-MINDED

The fight to defeat the Moors changed Spain forever. One of the most visible changes was the growth of a large, professional army. The Spanish government supported this highly trained fighting force. In many respects, the Spanish Army developed into a strong fighting force. Young boys, like Francisco Pizarro, did not study books, but warfare. They learned fighting tactics and how to use weapons. The Moors in southern Spain posed a real threat to the Spanish Christians. Since they were so close to the Moors, many Spaniards learned to fight. And because fighting was almost constant, many young Spaniards became skilled at waging war.

The Spanish developed new and effective tactics for warfare. Spanish infantrymen learned how to act in concert with one another. This allowed their infantry to attack an opposing force using complex maneuvers. Such tactics allowed the Spanish infantry to inflict much harm on their enemies.

Likewise, the Spanish cavalry possessed improved armor and weapons to enhance their fighting tactics. Armored men on horseback usually fought with metal swords. Sometimes, they carried lances as long as 14 feet. It is likely that the best riders in Europe during the fifteenth and sixteenth centuries were in the Spanish cavalry.

Other weapons included the crossbow and the harquebus (sometimes spelled arquebus). The crossbow was a heavy bow attached to a wooden base. A soldier used the weapon to fire an undersized arrow called a bolt. These projectiles inflicted great damage on opposing soldiers. The crossbows shot the bolts with so much energy that from several hundred yards (or meters) away, they could even pierce steel armor.

The harquebus was an early form of gun, perhaps best described as a light musket. To load these weapons, a soldier inserted a gunpowder charge. Then he pushed the bullet or ball into the barrel. He then rammed the bullet all the way down the barrel using a stick or a ramrod. To shoot these firearms, a fighter lowered a piece of burning fuse into the barrel. Then, the soldier waited for the fuse to ignite

This painting, by Lorenzo Lotto, shows a man with a harquebus. In the fifteenth century, the Spanish military used improved weaponry, like the harquebus, to enhance their tactics. The harquebus was an early form of gun, similar to a light musket.

the packed gunpowder charge. This process took time, and the weapon often misfired. Thus, these weapons had the disadvantages of a lengthy loading and firing process as well as unpredictability—especially in combat. But even with these weaknesses, weapons like the harquebus enabled the Spanish to inflict heavy casualties on opposing armies. Since the Inca had never seen firearms, these weapons intimidated the Indian forces. These kinds of weapons proved to be essential for the Spanish in fighting American Indians.

All of these techniques and weapons made it possible for the Spanish to win huge victories in the New World. Perhaps it was the longstanding military traditions that served as the most important aspect to Spanish military success in the Americas. After fighting against the Moors for so long, the Spanish acquired a reputation for military success and cruelty. Opposing armies feared Spanish ruthlessness on the battlefield.

Spanish culture supplied men of courage who seemed to fear nothing. The Spanish fighters relied upon their abilities and available resources in battle. Using their tactics and advanced weaponry, small numbers of Spanish soldiers conquered over-whelming numbers of American Indians. In some respects, the Spanish soldiers knew only to attack. Even when they were attacked, the Spanish would usually sound the battle cry of "*Santiago y a ellos!*" In English, this means, "*St. James and at them!*" Spain's patron saint is St. James. "*And at them*" meant to charge the enemy.

RELIGION AS A WEAPON

The Spanish often justified their wars as necessary to accomplish holy goals. Since they fought the Spanish Muslims, this makes sense. Religion became a very visible difference between the two sides. To unify their forces, the Spanish Christian kingdoms often relied upon their religion. War to gain control of the Iberian Peninsula became a fight to rid Spain of non-Christians. This attitude later included other non-Christians besides the Moors. Christianity became the focus of the Moor wars. Once this occurred, the Spanish began to use religion to control their defeated enemies.

To help them in their fight against the Moors, Ferdinand and Isabella set up a special court in

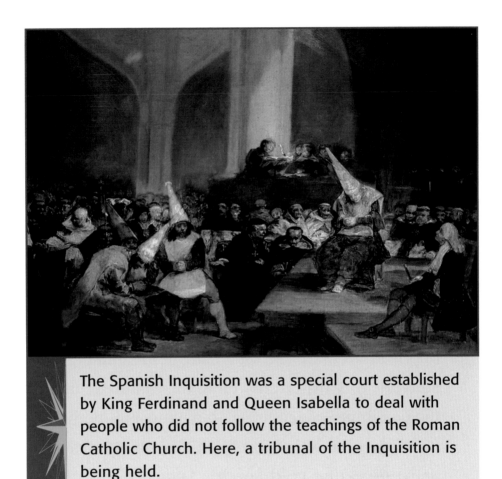

The Spanish Inquisition was a special court established by King Ferdinand and Queen Isabella to deal with people who did not follow the teachings of the Roman Catholic Church. Here, a tribunal of the Inquisition is being held.

1480 to deal with people who did not follow Roman Catholic teachings. This court was the Spanish Inquisition, which had the power to put people in prison or even put them to death. If individuals did not accept Christianity, they faced death. Pizarro later used this same structure against the Incan emperor.

GOLD, SLAVES, AND MISSION WORK

After defeating the Moors, the Spanish shifted their fight elsewhere. Until their victory, Spain had been intent on ridding the Iberian Peninsula of all Muslims. Now that their homeland was secure against non-Christian threats, the Spanish redirected their energies to conquer and convert other people. Within just a few years of Columbus's initial voyage across the Atlantic, it soon became clear that a land of opportunity awaited brave souls. The so-called New World seemed to offer two great opportunities for the Spanish: gold and possible converts to Christianity. First, the Spanish realized the possibility of acquiring gold almost immediately. Columbus himself reported on this when he saw the natives wearing gold jewelry "attached to holes in their noses."[8] Using signs to communicate with the natives, Columbus learned that the gold had come from the south. He also found out that a ruler in the south had so much of the precious metal that he ate and drank from golden plates and cups.[9]

Besides gold, Columbus foresaw another way to profit from the natives in the New World: slavery. Columbus observed that the Indians were "fit to be ordered about and made to work." [10] Later Spanish explorers placed many American Indians into slavery to enrich themselves.

Columbus also saw the potential for Catholic mission work in the New World. He wrote, "I believe they would readily become Christians, for they seem to have no religion." [11] For many conquistadors, this report justified conquering "pagan" peoples. Most of the early Spanish military expeditions included priests to convert the local natives.

Columbus hoped to become rich by finding the rumored gold. But the explorer never discovered much gold for himself or his Spanish supporters. Instead, his stories motivated younger, more ambitious men from Spain. Stories of gold, land, and unconverted Indians spread throughout Spain. Thousands of Spanish men listened and dreamed of what might be in the New World. Thousands of Spanish men wished to find gold, conquer land, acquire slaves, and convert the natives to Catholicism. And thousands of Spanish men eventually left their homeland to follow their dreams in the New World. One of these men was Francisco Pizarro.

Test Your Knowledge

1 What was the prime motivation for explorers like Columbus?

  a. To ensure naval supremacy for Spain

  b. To find an all-sea trade route to the Far East

  c. To expand the slave trade

  d. None of the above

2 What effect did battling the Moors have on the Spanish military?

  a. The Spanish began to use new weapons like the crossbow.

  b. The Spanish improved their cavalry's armor and tactics.

  c. The Spanish developed a more coordinated infantry.

  d. All of the above.

3 What was a harquebus?

  a. An early gun, like a musket

  b. A navigational tool

  c. A type of sailing ship

  d. A tool for map-making

4 What was the Spanish Inquisition?

a. A committee created by King Ferdinand to review new plans for global exploration

b. A group of Spanish nobles who decided how the country's money would be spent

c. A court designed to deal with those who did not accept the Roman Catholic faith

d. None of the above

5 Why did Columbus believe that the native people of the Americas would readily convert to Christianity?

a. Because he was prepared to force them at gunpoint

b. Because they could be bribed into converting

c. Because, to him, they seemed to have no religion of their own

d. None of the above

ANSWERS: 1. b; 2. d; 3. a; 4. c; 5. c

Pizarro's Early Experience in the New World

PIZARRO GOES TO THE NEW WORLD

In 1502, Pizarro left Spain for the New World. He wanted to get rich and become famous. Because he had heard stories of great wealth, Pizarro decided he would go to the Spanish colonies in the New World. Pizarro was convinced that he could become wealthy by conquering one of the native empires in the Americas. He went to Hispaniola (the island that today is Haiti and the Dominican Republic). Pizarro's second cousin, Hernándo Cortés, was supposed to leave Europe on the same ship. Because of an injury, Cortés stayed in Spain. He later went to the New World and conquered the Aztecs of Mexico. As for Pizarro, little is known about his activities for about seven years.

On November 10, 1509, Pizarro set sail for unexplored lands in South America with Alonzo de Ojeda. Ojeda had gone with Columbus on his second voyage to the New World. Ojeda became the governor of the Spanish territory in northern South America in 1508. His territory included the city of Cartagena, located on an island off the coast of modern Colombia (and also part of Colombia). Ojeda decided to bring Pizarro with him as he established control and searched for gold.

Ojeda, Pizarro and their force of about 70 men arrived ready to fight at the village of Turbago, Colombia. Reaching their destination, the Spaniards realized that the Indian community had deserted. Since the Europeans wanted gold, they went farther inland to look for Indian treasure. Unfortunately for Ojeda and his men, it was a trap. The natives attacked the Spanish, who were scattered and disorganized. The Indians killed many of Ojeda's force with poison-tipped arrows. Ojeda and Pizarro were two of the fortunate few who survived. Even they nearly perished, but the few men who stayed on the ship discovered the men and attacked the Indians. After Ojeda's rescue, he raised another small army and retaliated by killing the women and children in Turbago.

The next year, 1510, Ojeda and Pizarro again conducted expeditions to South America in present-day Colombia. Ojeda built a fort on the coast, on the Gulf of Uraba. He and his small force left the protection of the fort to find Indian gold. Instead of finding gold, he and his men found Indians firing poison-tipped arrows at them. They quickly returned to the safety of the fort's walls.

PIZARRO SERVES AS LEADER

Ojeda then received reinforcements from Panama. With a larger force, the Spaniards managed to keep the Indians from openly attacking their settlement. After that, Ojeda founded the town of San Sebastian. Those who lived there struggled to survive. They lacked the necessary food supplies, and the local Indians frequently attacked. Ojeda decided to leave to find reinforcements and supplies. He placed Pizarro in charge of San Sebastian. Governor Ojeda ordered Pizarro to hold out for two months. If the governor did not return within those two months, Pizarro was to leave San Sebastian with the small armed force that remained.

Ojeda was unable to get the necessary men and supplies to strengthen San Sebastian. After waiting two months, Pizarro set sail for the larger port at Cartagena. At Cartagena, Pizarro found the reinforcements bound for San Sebastian. The relief forces were led by Martín Fernández d'Enciso. Pizarro joined the relief force and returned to San Sebastian. There, the Spaniards found the fort destroyed. The relief force endured several Indian attacks, which led to a dispute between Enciso and Pizarro. Enciso wanted to stay at the settlement, while Pizarro believed the group should return to Cartagena. The argument escalated nearly to the point of a duel between the two men. Finally, another member of the group intervened. His name was Vasco Núñez de Balboa, who recommended that the group begin a new settlement in another area on the Gulf of Uraba. Balboa had gone to the area a few years before. He thought the area to be safer since the natives there did not use poison-tipped arrows.

Following Balboa's advice, the group sailed to another coastline on the Gulf of Uraba. Enciso, Pizarro, Balboa, and their force set up Santa Maria de la Antigua del Darien. Enciso was named the governor. Sadly, he lacked the skills to lead the new colony effectively. After a time, many of the men chose Balboa to replace Enciso. Pizarro was named the garrison commander. But under Spanish law, the king or his representative appointed the governor, not the men under the governor. Enciso felt cheated and returned to Spain to plead his case before the king. The king appointed a new governor who ordered Balboa's arrest.

THE EXPEDITION FROM DARIEN

Balboa left Darien in 1513, before the replacement

governor and arrest warrant arrived. Pizarro and his soldiers went with Balboa, who headed west. This expedition had two purposes. First, Balboa wanted to learn if the rumors of gold in the area were true. Second, the local Indians had described a great sea, perhaps a water route to valuable trade with the East Indies. In Balboa's day, most explorers did not realize that two large continents lay between Europe and the East Indies. Thus, many of the early explorations hoped to find an easy sea route to the East Indies. This was the case for Balboa and Pizarro in the Darien expedition. Balboa and his group landed on the east coast of Central America and crossed the Panamanian isthmus. The isthmus, the narrowest strip of land in the Americas, separates the Atlantic and Pacific Oceans.

The 45-mile trip was difficult and filled with many dangers. The expedition had to pass through jungles and cross mountains. Tropical heat and humidity spoiled food supplies and ruined the metal armor and equipment. Disease weakened and killed many of the men. After 24 grueling days, the men finally reached the other side of the isthmus.

Then they set about exploring the area. In particular, Balboa wanted to see if the rumors of the so-called South Sea (Pacific Ocean) were true. After setting up a camp at the base of a hill, Balboa climbed the hill alone. From the top of the hill, in September 1513, Balboa became the first known European to see the Pacific Ocean. Calling from the hilltop, he cried out to his companions to follow him.

The whole group then climbed the hill and approached the Pacific Ocean together. Balboa led them, carrying a Spanish flag as he entered the water. Then he raised his sword into the air, and declared that the great ocean and any land it touched belonged to Spain. Balboa became the first European to touch the Pacific Ocean.

Balboa made another discovery while camped near the ocean: pearls. He and his men maintained good relations with the local Indians. To show their goodwill toward the Spaniards, the natives presented Balboa with more than 200 pearls. He learned that the pearls came from sea oysters. Balboa then established the settlement of San Miguel. He hoped the town would help in the

The explorer Vasco Núñez de Balboa is shown discovering the Pacific Ocean in September 1513. Francisco Pizarro was a part of this expedition. A few years later, Pizarro was ordered to arrest his friend Balboa.

development of pearl fisheries in the area. The explorer expected the pearls to make him wealthy and enrich the king of Spain.

Unfortunately for Balboa, the king's new governor of Darien arrived while he was discovering the Pacific Ocean and establishing San Miguel. The new governor, Pedro Arias de Avila (usually known as Pedrarias) appointed Francisco Pizarro to be captain

(continued on page 48)

The *Encomienda* System

S panish settlers in the New World often treated the Indians as slaves. Columbus had earlier recognized "how easy it would be to convert these people—and to make them work for us."[*] Landowners soon showed how easy it was—even though it was illegal under Spanish law.

Spain established the *encomienda* system, which was like a trusteeship. This meant that when a conquistador defeated a group of people, those people then gave land and towns to the conquistador. Under Spanish law, the conquistador or *encomendero* could tax the people. These taxes were usually in the form of labor. Thus, a conquistador might require the local townspeople to give a certain amount of time working for him, or require them to complete a certain project. The *encomendero*, as the trustee, also had obligations in this system. Spanish law required the conquistadors to protect the local people. Usually, they provided protection by maintaining a small army. These armies allowed the Spanish to maintain control over the local Indians. The conquistadors also were required to offer religious teachings to the natives.

Sadly, the *encomienda* system resulted in virtual slavery for the Indian population. Officially, the Spanish crown did not authorize slavery in the

New World. But the *encomienda* system looked a lot like slavery. The landowners controlled many parts of the lives of the natives on their properties. This working class lived in poverty and enjoyed few rights. These poor natives were peasants. Many of the landowners were ambitious and power-hungry men. In the name of stability, the Spanish government banned natives from living on Spanish land. The natives still owed labor to the *encomenderos*, but they could not live on the actual *encomienda*. However, most Spanish landowners abused the system.

Landowners forced Indians living in the area to search for gold, silver, and other precious metals. If they found anything of value, the Spaniards claimed it for themselves. If the natives were unable to provide the required amount of labor, the penalties usually included the loss of what little land they owned. Thus, the Spanish landowners gained more and more land while the native Indians lost land and power to the Spanish ruling class. Besides the land abuses, the Spanish sometimes treated native women very badly. Often, the *encomienda* system was slavery in everything but name. It exists under other names in Latin America today.

* Morison, Samuel Eliot, *The European Discovery of America: The Southern Voyages*, A.D. *1492–1616* (New York: Oxford University Press, 1974), 67.

(continued from page 45)

of the governor's soldiers. Not long afterward, Pizarro followed orders and arrested his friend and companion, Vasco Núñez de Balboa. Pedrarias charged the discoverer of the Pacific Ocean with treason for illegally replacing Enciso as governor of Darien. After his conviction, Balboa was beheaded in 1519.

Pizarro continued to serve under Governor Pedrarias. In 1515, Pedrarias sent Pizarro to trade with natives living along the Pacific coast. There, Pizarro eagerly listened to stories of a land where people ate and drank from plates and cups of gold and silver. The tales seemed unbelievable, but Pizarro accepted them. He was determined to go to this land with such great wealth.

PIZARRO THE LANDOWNER

Pizarro also helped the Spanish authorities gain and keep control in Panama. After the capital was moved to Panama, Pizarro helped subdue some rebellious Indian tribes near there. In return for his service, Pizarro received a large piece of land. Spanish settlers referred to any large piece of property given by the governor within his colony

In this painting by Diego Rivera, Indian slaves work on a sugar plantation. Under the *encomienda* system, a conquistador who defeated a group of people would receive land from them and could tax the people, often in the form of labor. The system resulted in virtual slavery for the Indians.

as an *encomienda*. Since natives still lived on the land granted to Pizarro, he received the benefits of their labor. Such workers received little pay for their labor.

Pizarro owned a large piece of property. He raised cattle on his land. He enjoyed a comfortable life of luxury. But the conqueror-to-be wanted more. He wanted gold. He wanted fame. He wanted more land. He wanted more power. Francisco Pizarro wanted to conquer an empire. And in 1522, he set about doing just that.

Test Your Knowledge

1 Who was Alonzo de Ojeda?

   a. A wealthy Spanish nobleman
who funded Pizarro's explorations

   b. A rival who sought to destroy Pizarro's
reputation

   c. Governor of the Spanish territory in
northern South America

   d. None of the above

2 What happened to Ojeda's first expedition
to Turbago?

   a. He and Pizarro defeated the local
Indians and found gold.

   b. He and Pizarro barely escaped with
their lives and found no gold.

   c. The Indians received the Spaniards
as friends.

   d. None of the above.

3 What gift did the local Indians of the Pacific
coast give Balboa?

   a. Gold and silver masks

   b. Rare spices and herbs

   c. Pearls

   d. None of the above

4 Why was Balboa beheaded?

   a. He refused to yield ownership of the
      lands he discovered to Spain.

   b. He tried to kill Pizarro.

   c. He hijacked a Spanish ship to aid his
      explorations.

   d. He committed treason by ousting Enciso
      as governor of Darien.

5 What was an *"encomienda"*?

   a. A system by which the Spanish
      government rewarded conquistadors

   b. A trusteeship that gave successful
      Spanish warriors ownership of land

   c. A system that resulted in virtual
      slavery for many Indians conquered
      by the Spanish

   d. All of the above

ANSWERS: 1. c; 2. b; 3. c; 4. d; 5. d

More Failures

PIZARRO'S FIRST ATTEMPT TO REACH THE INCA

Pizarro believed a southern land with much gold existed. Many other Spaniards did not. In 1522, Pizarro made an agreement with two other Spaniards interested in acquiring great wealth from the natives of South America. With the approval of Governor

Francisco Pizarro, Diego de Almagro, and Hernando de Luque were partners in a company formed to conquer lands south of Panama and acquire riches there. This picture portrays the signing of the agreement among the three men. Eventually, Almagro and Pizarro would have a bitter falling-out.

Pedrarias, Pizarro formed a company with Diego de Almagro and Hernando de Luque. The purpose was to conquer the territory south of Panama and obtain gold and riches. Diego de Almagro was a soldier of fortune who happened to be in Panama. Hernando de Luque was a Spanish priest who desired to bring his religious beliefs to the unconverted people of Peru. Father Luque also enjoyed "considerable influence" in Panama and was trusted by those with money.[12] Few people thought the new company could achieve its goals. Some Panamanians believed the three to be crazy.

Despite the doubts of area residents, the three partners managed to raise the funds needed for the ambitious expedition. The three divided the duties of managing the company's forces. Pizarro was named the head of the expedition, and Almagro was charged with providing the equipment and supplies to be transported by ships. Meanwhile, Luque agreed to stay in Panama and run the company. The three also decided that Luque needed to keep up a good working relationship with Pedrarias to maintain the governor's support for their undertaking.

Pizarro's first expedition to Peru began in November 1524. He set sail from the west coast of Panama with four horses and 114 volunteers. They sailed south and eventually reached present-day

Colombia. Almagro was supposed to follow in a smaller ship as soon as he had enough equipment and provisions. This first attempt to conquer Peru was anything but successful. Pizarro had "embarked at the worst time of the year for a voyage south—the rainy season."[13] Pizarro faced strong winds, fierce storms, and rough seas.

Pizarro finally reached the coast, but instead of cities to conquer, he and his men found only swamplands and dense forests. The men suffered in oppressive heat. Finding nothing to conquer, Pizarro and his men continued sailing along the coast. Occasionally they made contact with small settlements. The sight of the large ship and strangers scared many of the Indians. Thus, Pizarro entered mostly empty villages. These small settlements kept them alive. He and his hungry men plundered the villages of food and a little bit of gold—some small trinkets.

Meanwhile, Almagro followed in another ship. He went as far as Rio de San Juan (what is now Cauca, Colombia) before turning back. Although he found more gold, he also ran into more resistance. On one occasion, an Indian spear struck

Almagro during an attack. He survived, but he lost an eye. Failing to find Pizarro, Almagro sailed back to the port of Chicamá, which was not far from Panama.

Pizarro managed to reach Punta Quemada, on the coast of present-day Colombia. After losing many of his men to disease, fatigue, and starvation, Pizarro decided to go to Chicamá. There, Pizarro and Almagro reunited. From Chicamá, Pizarro sent his treasurer back to Panama with a small amount of gold to give an account to Governor Pedrarias. The gold Pizarro sent was all he had managed to acquire on this first attempt to find riches. Mostly, what the expedition found was only wet swamps and venomous snakes. What little gold they had found "failed to pay for the expedition or to impress Panama's adventurers." [14] Reluctantly, Pizarro and Almagro decided to return to Panama.

But Pizarro, Almagro and Father Luque did not give up their dreams of finding wealth and spreading Catholicism. Instead, they immediately made plans for another expedition. Of course, to realize their goals, they needed more money, more men, and more supplies.

A SECOND TRY

Pizarro's second expedition to Peru left Panama in 1526. This time, Pizarro had 160 men, a few horses, and two ships. This expedition went farther south than any other expedition had before it. Pizarro and his men found more Indians and gold. More important, the Indians shared tales of a great city in the mountains. They claimed this city was filled with gold.

Despite the promising signs, it seemed that Pizarro might fail before he could begin. Resistance to Pizarro's plans came from a powerful person. Governor Pedrarias was opposed to Pizarro, Almagro and Luque gathering together another expedition because Pedrarias wanted to take a force to Nicaragua and was also in need of volunteers. Although it took some time for the men to gain Pedrarias's backing for another expedition, the governor eventually agreed to support them. Later, when a new governor, Pedro de los Rios, arrived from Spain, Luque managed to befriend him.

On March 10, 1526, Pizarro, Almagro and Luque signed an agreement in which they agreed to divide equally all the territory that was captured and all the gold, silver, and jewels found. The partners bought two ships, with Pizarro and Almagro sailing together to the mouth of the San Juan River. Here they separated, with Pizarro commanding a group of soldiers on the mainland while Almagro set out for Panama to gather more supplies and volunteers. The second ship was placed under the command of another member of the expedition, Bartolomé Ruiz, who sailed south, reaching as far as Punta de Pasados. There, Ruiz made many observations and collected much information before returning to Pizarro. Upon his return, he discovered that Pizarro and his men had endured a great deal of suffering.

Almagro and Luque finally managed to soothe the governor's fears about Pizarro and the series of mistakes their company had made. The governor allowed the two to send a ship to Pizarro, but his permission was restricted to a ship with only enough men to sail it. Thus, the ship contained few provisions and no reinforcements. And the ship also carried orders that Pizarro was required to return to Panama.

Pizarro was not pleased when he learned that the governor wanted him to call off the expedition. Instead of obeying the governor's orders, Pizarro angrily refused to leave. Only 13 followers stayed with him. The 14 Spaniards stood on the

A Line in the Sand

In 1526, a ship arrived with orders from the governor of Panama to take Francisco Pizarro back to Panama. Pizarro, however, was in no mood to return to the Spanish colony without first seeing the rich country he had learned about from the local Indians. The ship's commander insisted that the starving and undersupplied men board the ship. What happened next helped spell the doom of the Incan Empire.

As they stood on the beach Pizarro dramatically drew a sword and made a line in the sand. The line ran east to west. He drew himself up and faced south. Then he declared, "Friends and comrades, on that side are toil, hunger, nakedness, the drenching storm, desertion, and death. On this side, ease and pleasure."* Then, still facing toward Peru, he proclaimed, "Choose, each man, what beach and watched the ship sail for Panama. They did not know then that they would be left alone to fend for themselves for several months. The land could not sustain them. The men faced hunger and the fear of local Indians becoming hostile. So they

best becomes a brave [Spaniard]. For my part, I go to the south."** Then, to show his disobedience to the governor's orders and his desire to continue on to Peru, Pizarro stepped across the line. Pizarro was already more than 50 years old. Despite his age, he chose a life that was difficult for much younger and stronger men. Pizarro still wished to claim land for Spain and find gold.

Despite his bravery and bold statements, most of Pizarro's men were tired of the hardship. Only 13 of his companions followed him across his line in the sand. The rest wanted to return to Panama. But the 13 who followed Pizarro across that line in the sand later became very wealthy when they conquered the Inca Empire.

* William H. Prescott, *History of the Conquest of Peru: With a Preliminary View of the Civilization of the Incas* (New York: A.L. Burt Company, n.d.), 200.
** Ibid.

made a large raft and sailed to the nearby island of Gorgona. There, they found enough game to prevent starvation.

Finally, after months of waiting, a ship appeared. The men were relieved to see it. When it arrived, Pizarro learned that it was not full of reinforcements. Instead, the ship had come to take them home. Pizarro was permitted to explore for six months before returning to Panama. The men sailed southward and scouted the coast. Pizarro went around the coast of present-day Ecuador before heading toward the city of Tumbez (in present-day northern Peru). Here, the natives proved to be friendly, so he continued making his way south along the coast. As they sailed near the coast, they observed the great Incan roads from the ship. Coastal natives spoke of a powerful and rich monarch who ruled the territory. Pizarro was convinced more than ever that this was the golden kingdom he first heard about years before.

The Spaniards, under strict orders from Pizarro, were well behaved. The Indians throughout the region warmly received the Spaniards. Pizarro did not want to do anything that might jeopardize his expedition and the chance to obtain riches. He knew that victory might be made easier if he kept up the appearance of friendship.

After sailing near the Incan coast, Pizarro was satisfied that he had finally found the empire he hoped to conquer. The aging Spaniard finally returned to Panama to make his report. He brought a few Indians, some gold, and llamas to prove his story. Despite the evidence of gold, his bright report, and his optimistic views of the opportunities, the governor was not impressed with his "cheap display of gold and silver toys and a few Indian sheep." [15] He stated that he "had no desire to build up other states at the expense" of Panama. [16] Then, the governor angrily denied Pizarro, Almagro, and Father Luque permission to continue their efforts.

Pizarro could not believe it. Finally he had proof of a vast and rich kingdom, but the governor would not support them in their quest. The three partners were convinced that wealth and power awaited them in South America. But they had spent all of their money on the two failed expeditions. They managed to borrow enough money to pay for one trip to Spain. They hoped to argue their case before the king, Emperor Charles V. Since they only had the funds for one of them to make the trip, they decided that Pizarro alone would appeal the governor's decision in Spain.

Almagro and Father Luque did not completely trust Pizarro, however. They knew that Pizarro was impressive and might be able to secure financing from the crown. But since neither Almagro nor Father Luque were going with the explorer, there were no guarantees that he would protect their interests as well. Father Luque advised Pizarro to remember their partnership while in Spain. The priest told his partners, "God grant, my children, that one of you may not defraud the other of his blessing!" [17]

PIZARRO SEES CHARLES V

Pizarro arrived in Seville in 1528 and was immediately taken into custody and thrown into jail. His old enemy, Martín Fernández d'Enciso, was responsible for his imprisonment. Enciso accused Pizarro of owing him money from the 1513 Darien expedition. Fortunately for Pizarro, Charles V had already heard the rumors of Inca gold and commanded Enciso to release the explorer.

In 1529, Pizarro received permission from Emperor Charles V to occupy Peru. Charles made Pizarro a knight and named him governor of Peru and captain-general of the expedition.

Pizarro made his way to Toledo. There, the emperor received him warmly. Charles was enticed by the tales of gold and the promise of new lands for his empire. Thus, Pizarro persuaded him to support their venture, and on June 26, 1529, the emperor laid down various powers in a signed agreement between the two. This agreement was called a *capitulation*. In this agreement, Charles made

Pizarro a knight. He also appointed Pizarro governor of Peru (New Castile) and captain-general of the expedition. From the earnings in Peru, Pizarro was supposed to receive a large salary. In addition, he was given absolute power and authority to rule any lands he might find and conquer. His governmental powers were to be separate and independent from the government of Panama and were granted to him in perpetuity (forever). More important, these powers guaranteed Pizarro that he and his partners did not need the approval or permission of the governor of Panama—they now had the approval and permission of the emperor himself and the independence to proceed as they saw fit. The new governor of Peru agreed to take 250 soldiers with him, as well as all the boats, munitions, and supplies necessary for such a large expedition.

Almagro and Father Luque received much less than their partner. Almagro became the "commander of the fortress of Tumbez," the Incan port city.[18] He also received a salary, but a much lower one than given to Pizarro. Father Luque was made Bishop of Tumbez, awarded an annual salary, and named "Protector of the Indians of Peru."[19]

READY TO BECOME CONQUISTADORS

Pizarro left Seville on January 18, 1530. He set sail with far fewer men than required under the capitulation, which called for him to take 250 armed men. He had failed to recruit enough men. So, to avoid detection by the Spanish authorities, he left at night. His half-brothers Hernando, Juan, and Gonzalo accompanied him. Each of the four Pizarro siblings would play an important role in the discovery, conquest, and establishment of Peru.

After arriving in Panama, Pizarro was forced to appease his two partners, who had not received the powers or titles that he had managed to secure for himself in Spain. He failed to mend the differences adequately. Later, the relationship between Pizarro and Almagro deteriorated into open conflict. Pizarro's quest for gold would end his friendship with Almagro. But the prospect of gold overshadowed their differences for a time. The three quickly made preparations for the upcoming expedition.

In early January 1531, Pizarro left Panama with 180 men and 27 cavaliers in three ships. His partners Almagro and Luque remained in Panama to raise more supplies and enlist additional troops.

Pizarro landed in the Bay of San Mateo, located near the mouth of the Santiago River. From there, the explorer and his forces began surveying the coast on foot. The three ships that brought them to the bay were then sent back to Panama. Pizarro ordered them to return with Almagro, additional supplies, and reinforcements. Pizarro and his men turned their attention to the Incan Empire.

Test Your Knowledge

1 Which of the following best characterizes Pizarro's first expedition to Peru?
   a. A stunning success, yielding a treasure trove of Inca gold
   b. A surprising success, yielding new treaties with local Indian tribes
   c. Basically a failure, though the explorer found a few gold trinkets
   d. None of the above

2 What obstacle confronted Pizarro's second expedition to Panama?
   a. Governor Pedrarias opposed the expedition.
   b. Pizarro could not get volunteers willing to endure Indian attacks.
   c. Pizarro could not find seaworthy vessels.
   d. None of the above.

3 What did Pizarro bring to the governor of Panama to support his idea that the empire of gold was near?
   a. A few gold items
   b. A few of the local Indians
   c. A few llamas
   d. All of the above

4 How did Charles V answer Pizarro's request for another expedition?

a. Charles forbade Pizarro to explore any further.

b. Charles agreed to fund Pizarro, knighted the explorer, and made him territorial governor of what is now Peru.

c. Charles permitted further expeditions but would not fund Pizarro.

d. None of the above.

5 When Pizarro drew his famous "line in the sand," how many men agreed to stay with the explorer?

a. His entire crew

b. About half his crew

c. Only 13 men

d. None of the above

ANSWERS: 1. c; 2. a; 3. d; 4. b; 5. c

The Inca Before Pizarro's Conquest

A VAST EMPIRE

The Inca Empire in the early sixteenth century, just before Pizarro's conquest, was one of the most advanced civilizations in the world. The empire relied on a large system of roads that connected the major cities with one another. At the time of the Spanish conquest, the Inca road system contained over 14,000 miles of roads.[20] The system featured two main roads. One of these ran parallel to the coast. The other, a highland road, ran through the mountains. The coastal road began in the north, near the present-day border with Ecuador. The main part of this road then ran south all the way to Arequipa or just west of Lake Titicaca in southern Peru. Other portions of the coastal road crossed the Chilean desert. The highland road connected northern Ecuador with Argentina, connecting much of the continent. These roads were vitally important. They allowed for better communication between the different cities and parts of the empire. They also served to remind conquered peoples and loyal subjects of Incan power. Although the Inca inherited the road system from earlier ruling groups, they invested a great deal of energy and resources into maintaining their roads. They also added to the system by building new roads into several regions of their empire.

The Inca built their roads with their technology in mind. Since the Inca did not have wheels or wheeled vehicles, traveling instead by foot, their roads often followed the steep slopes of the countryside.[21] The roads were uneven. Sometimes the roads were little more than a path. In other places, the roads were very wide: as much as 82 feet.[22] Portions of the roads still exist today. "Generally, the road is wider where the land is flat, and narrower where it ascends or descends slopes."[23]

It took less than a century for the Incas to build their empire. This impressive achievement included the integration of various peoples under one government. This feat is even more amazing considering the vast and harsh terrain that made up Incan territory. Although the Inca experienced rebellions, they seemed to handle the details of governing a far-flung empire rather well. One of their strong suits lay in the way in which they dealt with local populations. Instead of using a single approach to govern conquered peoples, the Inca adapted their approach to the special conditions of a local situation.[24] Thus, the Inca used a variety of methods in ruling their empire.

INCAN GOVERNMENT

The Incas relied upon a dictatorship form of

Visitors today can still see the ruins of Machu Picchu, an ancient Incan city. The Inca had taken less than a century to build their empire, which, at its peak, covered 380,000 square miles and held over 16 million people.

government. This means that one ruler held virtually all the power in the government. This one ruler was the emperor. The Inca called their emperor *Sapa Inca*, which meant, "sole Inca."[25] In many ways, he was the sole Inca. He carried out the important functions of the Incan religion and government. The Inca viewed the Sapa Inca as the representative of the Sun. The emperor served as the head priest. He led the important religious festivals. He commanded the empire's armies. "He imposed taxes, made laws"[26] and appointed judges. "He was the source from which everything flowed."[27] Like European rulers who held almost all power, "all dignity, all power"[28] came from him.

To show his superiority, the Sapa Inca dressed in colorfully dyed clothing made of the finest wool. He also wore jewelry made of gold and precious stones. He wore a head-covering that included two feathers from a rare bird found only in the desert regions of the Incan Empire. Incan law protected these birds from hunting or captivity. The Inca reserved use of the feathers for the Sapa Inca's headdress.

INCAN RELIGION

Religion impacted much of an Incan's daily life. Many of the activities centered on their agricultural methods, their many deities, or the treatment of poor health and diseases. A large group of priests served to lead the Incans in these religious activities. This priest class guided the people in religious ceremonies and celebrations.[29] Even the Sapa Inca relied on the expertise of the priests: rarely did the

This picture depicts the Incas consecrating offerings to the Sun. The Incas considered their emperor, the Sapa Inca, to be the representative of the Sun.

emperor make decisions without seeking advice from the priests. The Inca believed that their gods told the priests what to do. The priests then gave the gods' blessing to the planned action. Generally, the more important government actions required very elaborate religious ceremonies.

Although the ruling class looked to the priestly class for spiritual guidance and advice, the priests also relied on the success of the ruling class. The class of priests depended upon the rest of society to supply them with their basic needs: food, shelter, and clothing.

When the Spaniards arrived in Peru, they brought with them their views of non-Christian religions. Just as their people had driven the Spanish Muslims from Spain, many of the early Spanish explorers wanted to drive out the local religions and replace them with Christianity. Many of the invaders believed the native religions to be "evil."[30] They thought that any religions other than their own were "devil worship."[31] This helps explain why they worked so hard to get rid of the Incan religious beliefs and practices. Since the Spanish wanted to explain why they ended the native practices, they often wrote a lot about the Incan religion. Historians now know about many of the Incan religious beliefs from these writings.

SEEDS FOR THE FALL OF THE INCA EMPIRE

Huayna Capac was the 12th Sapa Inca. His people called him "The Young Chief Rich in Virtues."[32] Under his leadership, the Inca extended their empire. His empire stretched from south of modern-day Santiago, Chile (in the south) to Quito, Ecuador (in the north). South of their empire lay land that was not fit to inhabit. Dense and difficult jungles seemed to protect the Inca on the east and north sides of their empire. And the Pacific Ocean served as the western border for the Inca. The vast Incan Empire held some 380,000 square miles and over 16 million people.[33] Not surprisingly, the Inca referred to their empire as the "Land of the Four Quarters." This basically meant *the world*. The Incas believed that they had conquered all of the known cultures. In the Inca world, there was nothing left to conquer—at least as far as they knew. But certain omens appeared to point to bad luck or bad things that would happen to the Inca and their empire.

These omens included many natural events. The Inca mistook these events to mean that their empire was destined to fall. These so-called omens included a large green comet visible in the night sky. Lightning struck the home of Huayna Capac. Since the Sapa Inca and his advisors knew the prophecies, they came to view virtually every act or event as bad news. To prevent panic, Huayna did not tell his subjects of the prophecy until the end of his life.

Huayna Capac's reign was also marked by personal tragedy. Keeping the tradition of all Sapa Inca before him, Huayna married his sisters. Through these wives, Huayna had several sons. But the Sapa Inca also married the daughter of a conquered chief from Quito. This princess became Huayna's favorite wife. He loved her so much that when she died, he moved to her hometown, Quito. This favoritism later led to a civil war that weakened the Inca Empire.

Soon, the Incas faced strange outsiders visiting their lands. These visitors had lighter colored skin, beards, and peculiar clothing. They brought strange, never-before-seen animals on which a man could ride—horses! These strangers also brought astonishing and powerful new weapons that made them seem almost unbeatable. The Inca, who viewed themselves as rulers of their known world, faced a new and powerful enemy who seemed determined to unseat the people of the sun.

Huayna Capac grew worried over the reports of these white-skinned strangers. He knew of an ancient prophecy that predicted the downfall of the Inca. The prophecy claimed that the time would come when the Inca would face "a people never before seen, who would destroy the religion and empire of the natives. . . . "[34]

To make matters worse for Huayna Capac, some of the Inca believed that the Spaniards were gods. They did not see them as great gods, but rather as servants of the Incan god of creation, Viracocha. The Incan word for the Spanish invaders was usually *viracochas.*

Unfortunately for the Inca, Huayna Capac did not live long enough to face the coming Spanish threat. An epidemic of smallpox, a European disease, wiped out many Inca from 1525 to 1527. (Smallpox spread to Mexico from Hispaniola in 1520. The disease then spread down to the northern regions of South America. From there, natives became infected throughout the Incan Empire.) Most of the Spaniards had already survived some form of the disease when they were children. When people survive a disease like smallpox, their body's immune system develops resistance to that disease, meaning the disease will probably never sicken a survivor again. The Inca and other peoples native to the Americas had never been exposed to smallpox. Thus, the Europeans had immunity against smallpox, but the Inca did not. The natives and Europeans often perceived the Europeans' natural immunity to such diseases as a kind of superiority. This mistaken belief helped the Europeans defeat the natives throughout the Americas.

The smallpox epidemic spread rapidly through the Incan empire. Huayna Capac himself fell ill and believed he would die. He called all of his advisors together and predicted that the Spaniards would come to rule his people. He said, "The reign of the 12 Incas ends with me. I can therefore certify to you that these people will return shortly after I shall have left you, and that they will accomplish what our father the Sun predicted they would: They will conquer our Empire, and they will become its only lords."[35] He also told his followers that when the Spaniards came back, "their weapons will be more powerful and invincible than yours."[36] Sadly, Huayna Capac also realized that the invaders were "strong, powerful men, who will outstrip you in

(continued on page 84)

European Diseases and the Inca

The civil war between Huáscar and Atahualpa weakened the Incan Empire before Pizarro and his band of soldiers ever arrived in Peru. This internal strife was one reason for Pizarro's great success. But one of the main reasons for the struggle between the half-brothers was a very small thing. In fact, it was microscopic. It was disease that led to the civil strife within the empire. Specifically, smallpox devastated the empire from 1525 to 1527. The rich and powerful were not immune from this deadly disease. Even the emperor, Huayna Capac, became sick with smallpox and died. The struggle for control began soon after his death.

If smallpox killed so many Incas, why did Indian diseases not seem to be so deadly to the Europeans? There are many possible explanations. In part, the large population of European cities helped increase natural immunities to European diseases over time. But another, and perhaps the most important reason, involves the way in which humans first contracted a particular disease. Each of the most deadly diseases (including smallpox) all came from animals.* Europeans raised many kinds of domesticated animals in Europe. Throughout the Americas, there were only five domesticated animals (the turkey, the guinea pig, the llama/alpaca, the Muscovy duck, and the dog). Unlike cattle or sheep, these native animals did not live in the large herds that allowed for rapid spread of disease. The European invaders came to the New World with immunity due to living alongside animals that carried these diseases. Those same diseases, when introduced to the native population, proved deadly to the American Indians.

In the century or two after Columbus's arrival in the New World, the Indian population is estimated to have declined by about 95 percent.** Deadly diseases decimated the Inca Empire before Pizarro's arrival. Pizarro seized the opportunity and conquered a weakened empire—an empire damaged by an unseen germ.

* Jared Diamond, "The Arrow of Disease," *Discover*, (October 1992), 66.

** Ibid., 72.

(continued from page 81)

everything."[37] Although he did not live to see it, Huayna recognized that the Incan Empire was coming to an end.

Historians believe that the smallpox epidemics of the mid- to late- 1520s killed about 200,000 people just in and around Cuzco. In Quito, many Inca also died, including Huayna Capac. His death came at a difficult time for his people.

INTERNAL STRIFE WEAKENS
THE INCA EMPIRE

As Pizarro, Almagro, and Luque were making their plans for conquest, civil war weakened the Inca Empire. Usually, when a Sapa Inca died, his oldest son inherited the throne. The last great Inca ruler, Huayna Capac, died in 1525 and a fight for control soon developed. At first, his oldest son, Huáscar, became Sapa Inca. But Huayna Capac had a favorite son, a younger one, by his favorite wife. And Huayna Capac wanted this younger son, Atahualpa, to inherit the throne. Huáscar was crowned king at Cuzco, but Atahualpa commanded a huge army at Quito. Quito named Atahualpa its king.

At first, there was a shaky truce between the two brothers. In time, though, war broke out. Huáscar ruled from the capital city. Meanwhile, Atahualpa gained the support of the most gifted generals. The civil war was bloody and raged for several years. Finally, Atahualpa gained the upper hand and captured Huáscar after defeating him in a number of battles. Huáscar ended up as a prisoner to his younger brother. Huáscar might have expected mercy from Atahualpa, but instead he received cruelty. Atahualpa feared that Huáscar's family and supporters might continue to fight against his claim to the throne. So Atahualpa gathered all of Huáscar's family and ordered them executed in front of Huáscar. Then his brother again imprisoned Huáscar. Atahualpa's brutal methods proved effective in defeating his brother. Some said that his cruelty "toward his own blood, in the end, served the victory of his enemies."[38]

Atahualpa won the civil war and secured his claim to the Inca throne, but the infighting shook the empire. This civil strife greatly weakened the empire's fighting strength. Atahualpa controlled the empire, but one that was much weaker than his

Atahualpa secured his claim to the Inca throne after winning a civil war. After the death of the previous emperor, Huayna Capac, Atahualpa (shown here) fought his half-brother Huáscar for the crown.

father had ruled. And Atahualpa did not know that a new and determined group of outsiders was coming to undo his hard-fought victory. The leader of these outsiders, Francisco Pizarro, learned of the civil war. More important, he understood what a rare opportunity lay before him and his men: an opportunity to get rich, an opportunity to seize land for Spain, an opportunity for greatness.

Test Your Knowledge

1 Which of the following best describes the Incan roads?

    a. The Incan lands had only a few miles of roads and trails.

    b. The Incas designed their road system for ox carts and wagons.

    c. The Incan road system included two main roads: one along the coast and one through the mountains.

    d. None of the above.

2 What kind of government did the Incas have?

    a. A democratic system with representatives from each territory

    b. A dictatorship, ruled by an emperor who made laws and led armies

    c. A system of communal farms that shared power equally

    d. None of the above

3 Which of the following best describes the role of Incan priests?

    a. The Incan priests presided over religious ceremonies but had little to do with government.

    b. The priests were distrusted by the Incan emperor.

    c. The Incan priests readily converted to Christianity when the Spaniards arrived.

    d. None of the above.

4 Which of the following did the Incas
see as a bad omen for their empire?
a. A great flood
b. A food shortage
c. A green comet
d. None of the above

5 What European disease had the greatest
impact on the Incas?
a. Smallpox
b. Measles
c. Mumps
d. Influenza

ANSWERS: 1. c; 2. b; 3. d; 4. c; 5. a

The Conquest
of Peru

PREPARING TO MEET THE ENEMY

Inca territory included a variety of regions with different physical features and climates. The Incas irrigated the level land closest to the coast to produce food crops. Farther inland, the Inca also farmed in high mountain valleys. Between the coastal plains and the fertile valleys lay the Andes Mountains. Located within one of these high, fertile valleys was the Inca capital of Cuzco. In May 1532, Pizarro and his men made their way inland from the coastal plain. He left some of his men at a fort near the coast, to make contact with Almagro when he arrived. The tall Pizarro led the others into the mountains. As they traveled and talked with the natives, Pizarro learned more about the civil war between Atahualpa and Huáscar. As the Spaniards marched inland, Pizarro continued his earlier policy of maintaining friendly relations with the Indians. Friendly natives welcomed the Spaniards as they entered villages with gifts and food.

Pizarro and his men faced no opposition as they approached Cuzco. In fact, they passed several empty forts. Rather than oppose their mountain ascent, Atahualpa decided to wait for the Spanish force in Cuzco. Thus, he left the narrow mountain passes unguarded. Pizarro observed these passes and the Incan fortifications. He believed them to be impassable if defended. When Pizarro and his men reached the crest of the Cajamarca Valley on November 15, 1532, they saw the large sprawling city of Cajamarca. But they also saw an enormous Incan army of at least 50,000 soldiers.

After reaching the edge of the valley, Pizarro and his men waited for the rear guard to catch up. Then, the Spaniards stayed in strict order as they descended into the valley. The sight was somewhat overwhelming. One of Pizarro's men described the Indian camp with its thousands of tents as looking "like a very beautiful city."[39] There were so many tents that the Spaniards grew afraid. The Europeans never thought that the Inca could "have so many tents in such good order."[40] Pizarro's men were afraid. But they realized that retreat might be even more dangerous than pressing forward. They believed that if the Indians "sensed any weakness," the much larger native force would kill them all.[41] So the Spaniards kept their formation as they moved down the mountain into the city of Cajamarca.

Pizarro realized that his men needed great courage to overcome the tremendous odds facing him and his men. He decided to make contact with the Inca through two of his loyal and trusted officers. One was his brother Hernando Pizarro. The other was Hernando de Soto. The two gathered as much information as they could about the Incan army. They made their way to the center of the Indian camp to meet the emperor. The two Spaniards made an imposing impression as they rode their horses boldly into the Inca camp. Both wore their armor. The Sapa Inca received them, but he was not intimidated by them or their horses. De Soto and Hernando invited the Sapa Inca to visit Pizarro in Cajamarca the next day. He agreed to come, and the two returned to the Spanish camp.

Pizarro now had enough information with which to plan his next move. He and his men were staying in Cajamarca. The town had a square with buildings along three sides. A mud wall hemmed in the other side of the square. The only entrance to the square was a single gate on the open end of the square.[42] Pizarro made his plans, then he and his men went to sleep, perhaps a little confident and a little frightened of what might happen the next day.

CAPTURING THE EMPEROR

At dawn, Pizarro ordered the men to their places. Most of his men and all the cavalry remained hidden in the buildings surrounding the square.

Two small cannons, called falconets, were positioned to provide cover to the square. Pizarro and his men waited for several hours.

As they waited, Atahualpa took his time arriving. The day wore on, but the Sapa Inca and his large army still had not arrived. In mid-afternoon, the Inca horde finally began making its way toward the square. Then, it appeared that Pizarro's plans might fall apart. Atahualpa sent word that he would appear the next day. Pizarro sent back a message that told the emperor he had nothing to fear. He assured Atahualpa that "he would be received by him as a friend and brother."[43] He also told the Inca ruler that a great banquet had been prepared in his honor. That message and its reception proved to be crucial to Pizarro's plans. Atahualpa changed his mind and decided to enter the city. But he decided to leave his army behind. Instead, 6,000 of his nobles went with him; all were unarmed. The Incan emperor "did not know the character of the Spaniard."[44]

When Atahualpa and his group finally appeared in the square, the sun was setting. The square was full of servants and nobles, but Pizarro was not present. Instead of Pizarro, a priest, Father Vincente de Valverde, met Atahualpa. Father Valverde spoke with Atahualpa through a translator. He began scolding Atahualpa and the Inca for their religious beliefs and practices. The priest explained the popular Spanish view of Christianity at the time. He described how God created the world and mankind. He talked about the pope and how Pizarro and his men were authorized to spread the Catholic religion. He also gave the emperor a choice. The Inca could either submit to Christianity and Spanish rule or face armed punishment. This declaration was called the *requerimiento*. The king of Spain required all Spanish explorers to read it when first making contact with a tribe or people. The *requerimiento* required all Indians to accept Christianity and Spanish rule. Atahualpa responded by asking to see the priest's prayer book. After taking a quick look, the Sapa Inca threw the book down. Father Valverde was embarrassed. He was also angry and probably frightened.

He quickly backed away and returned to Pizarro's hiding place. There, he pleaded with Pizarro to punish the Sapa Inca for his insults. The priest asked Pizarro, "Do you not see that while

(continued on page 98)

Priests as Conquistadors

Although Spanish soldiers won great battles and conquered empires in the Americas, another group of Spaniards played an important role in the exploration and settlement of the Americas: Catholic priests. Usually, each Spanish army entering an unclaimed territory included at least one Roman Catholic priest who acted as a missionary. Sometimes, an expedition might include several priests. One reason these priests went with the armies was to provide spiritual guidance for them.

The main reason the Spanish missionaries went with the armies was to convert the natives to Christianity. These early Catholic missionaries set up small communities to minister to the Indians. These communities were called missions. At the missions, priests and other workers offered food, clothing, shelter, and religious teachings to Indians. And at the missions, Indians learned valuable information about raising livestock and new farming techniques. Usually, the Spanish missions offered more protection for Indians than they otherwise received at the hands of the Spanish.

Sometimes, the priests seemed more interested in conquering rather than converting the

Indians. After all, one of Pizarro's partners was Father Luque. Although he seemed genuinely interested in teaching the natives, he effectively ran the company for Pizarro and Almagro. And in Pizarro's expedition to Peru, it was Father Valverde who delivered the *requerimiento* (or requirement) to them. Usually, the leader of the expedition delivered the *requerimiento*, not the priest. And at the decisive battle in which Atahualpa was captured, it was also Father Valverde who gave approval to attack the unarmed Incas.

Pizarro followed the example of Hernándo Cortés, who conquered the Aztecs. Just as Cortés did, priests began converting natives to Christianity after an area came under Spanish control. Spaniards accepted those Incas who accepted Christianity. Indians who rejected the Catholic teachings faced mistreatment or even death. At the very least, unconverted Indians were considered dangerous to Spanish control.

Much like the conquistadors, Spanish priests reflected Spanish society. Religious unity ensured political unity. Spanish conquistadors carried both the sword and the cross with them as they brought Spanish culture to their American colonies.

(continued from page 95)

we stand here wasting our breath in talking with this dog . . . the fields are filling with Indians?"[45] Father Valverde gave his blessing to attack the Indians. Pizarro waved a white scarf to his men. They responded to the signal and attacked the unsuspecting natives.

What followed can hardly be called a battle. Instead, it was a massacre. Inca were slaughtered by the hundreds. Dead bodies blocked the only gate. Spanish bullets and crossbow bolts cut down Inca in the square. Mounted cavalry soldiers used their swords to slash and kill the fleeing and confused Inca. Pizarro, leading a small group of soldiers, made his way to Atahualpa. For a time, the Inca ruler was held on his litter as servant after servant bravely took the place of those struck down. But their attempts to protect him proved useless. A small group of Spaniards, led by Pizarro, seized Atahualpa and hauled him back to the houses on the square. The supreme ruler of the Inca, who claimed to be a descendant of the Sun God, was now a prisoner of Pizarro's small band of men.

The slaughter was almost beyond belief. The Spanish force of about 180 men managed to kill at

A print depicts a Spanish soldier grasping Atahualpa during a battle to capture him. Slain servants of the Inca king lie around him. In the battle, the Spanish killed at least 2,000 Incas, though the Indians said 10,000 of their people were killed.

least 2,000 Inca that day. (The Spanish estimated the dead at 2,000. Incan estimates were a much higher 10,000.) To the Incan survivors and the Spanish victors, "it was an extraordinary thing to see so great a ruler captured in so short a time."[46] Amazingly, the only Spaniard wounded was Pizarro. He was cut in the hand when he stopped a

Spanish soldier from killing Atahualpa. Much like Cortés, Pizarro seized control by killing many natives and capturing their ruler.

What made the slaughter even more appalling was that the Indians did not attack any of the Spaniards. Instead, they tried to hold their ground and protect their emperor. All this proved to be a wasted effort, however, as the Spaniards killed and wounded thousands of the virtually defenseless Indians. In less than a half-hour, Pizarro and his men had won a crushing victory over the mighty Incan force. The short battle was "long enough to decide the fate of Peru." [47]

The victory was amazing even to the Spaniards themselves. One of Pizarro's men claimed, "Truly, it was not accomplished by our own forces for there were so few of us. It was by the grace of God, which is great." [48]

A KING'S RANSOM

To hide his true intentions, Pizarro treated Atahualpa like royalty. He allowed his family to live with him. The captured ruler lived a life of luxury and comfort, even though he was a prisoner. Atahualpa

A woodcut image portrays Pizarro with Atahualpa. To mask his intentions, Pizarro treated Atahualpa well after his capture. The Inca leader continued to live a life of comfort.

even ate off his royal plates and drank from his royal cups—all made of gold. The royal prisoner learned a little Spanish and how to play chess. But Atahualpa feared that his brother, Huáscar, might again challenge his claim to the throne.

Atahualpa quickly realized that the Spanish valued gold. Thus, Atahualpa made Pizarro an appealing offer. In exchange for his freedom, the

The Incas collect gold for Atahualpa's ransom. Atahualpa offered Pizarro a room measuring 22 feet by 17 feet filled with gold, and two rooms filled with silver.

Sapa Inca promised to fill a 17- by 22- foot room, 9 feet high with gold. He also vowed to fill another room twice with silver. Pizarro was thrilled that, at last, he might become very wealthy. He agreed to Atahualpa's offer, but only if the payment was supplied within two months. Atahualpa immediately sent messengers throughout the empire to begin collecting gold and silver.

While in captivity, Atahualpa learned that his brother and rival to the throne, Huáscar, wanted to escape. Atahualpa realized this could cost him the throne. The Sapa Inca ordered Huáscar put to death. His guards drowned him in a river.[49]

About the same time, Diego de Almagro arrived at Cajamarca. Pizarro's partner brought with him 200 men, all wanting a share of the ransom. Almagro believed that Pizarro intended to cheat him out of his share of the loot. Pizarro welcomed his partner and the reinforcements. Now the conquistador had enough men to gather even more gold from the Incas.

Test Your Knowledge

1 The Incan capital of Cuzco was located

a. along the coast, in what is now Chile.

b. high in the Andes Mountains.

c. near the Amazon River.

d. none of the above.

2 Whom did Pizarro send into the Incan encampment?

a. A single scout

b. Two trusted officers, one of whom was Pizarro's brother

c. A small regiment of armed conquistadors

d. None of the above

3 How did Pizarro plan to kidnap the Incan emperor?

a. By defeating the Incas in battle

b. By seizing the emperor at night, while the Incan guards slept

c. By inviting the emperor to the Spanish encampment at Cajamarca

d. By splitting the navy between northern and southern harbors

4 How was Emperor Atahualpa treated
by the Spaniards?
   a. He was tortured and held in a
      small cell.
   b. He was chained to a tree.
   c. He was treated with respect and dignity.
   d. None of the above.

5 What was the ransom agreed to by Pizarro
and Atahualpa?
   a. A handful of gold and silver bars
   b. All the gold the Spaniards could carry
   c. A lifetime supply of healing herbs
      and spices
   d. A roomful of gold and two more of silver

ANSWERS: 1. b; 2. b; 3. c; 4. c; 5. d

Pizarro Struggles to Keep Control

THE EXECUTION OF ATAHUALPA

Now that Pizarro had received the ransom, he no longer needed Atahualpa. But one of Pizarro's most trusted men, Hernando de Soto, had grown fond of the Incan leader. Their friendship stood in the way of Pizarro getting rid of Atahualpa. De Soto persistently opposed any talk of killing Atahualpa. Executing Atahualpa was one of the few things on which Diego de Almagro and Pizarro agreed. Father Valverde also believed it necessary to kill Atahualpa. Pizarro acted deceitfully to satisfy Almagro and remove any possible threat that the Inca leader might pose. In late August, Governor Pizarro sent de Soto on a phony errand to find a rumored group of armed natives.

While de Soto was gone, Atahualpa's Spanish enemies acted boldly. First, they brought charges against the captive ruler. The governor formed a panel to judge the case. Pizarro appointed himself, Almagro, and Father Valverde to hear the case. A series of Indian witnesses came before the three judges. A dishonest translator served as interpreter for the court.

The charges against Atahualpa included many things accepted in Incan society. For instance, they charged the Sapa Inca with polygamy (having more than one wife). Since Incan custom required the Sapa Inca to have more than one wife, this charge seemed unfair. Another charge accused Atahualpa of promoting idolatry. Again, the charge was true, but only because of Incan religious practices. Perhaps the most serious charge Atahualpa faced involved his claim to the Incan throne. Incan law recognized only the appointed heir as legitimate. Therefore, even under Incan law Atahualpa's claim and war against his brother Huáscar was illegal. Since Pizarro himself claimed power in Peru through warfare, it seems unlikely that this charge was valid. Instead, it was just another possible excuse to get rid of the Incan ruler.

Some of the men did defend Atahualpa. They argued that since he was a sovereign ruler, only King Charles could judge his guilt or innocence. Perhaps word should be sent to the king to let him determine the matter. Sadly, these arguments did nothing to change the outcome. The panel continued to hear the charges. Then, it considered the charges against Atahualpa.

The verdict was never in doubt. Pizarro, Almagro, and Father Valverde found Atahualpa guilty of treason. He was sentenced to death. Atahualpa was to be burned alive. The verdict overwhelmed the conquered ruler. Upon hearing the sentence, Atahualpa asked Pizarro, "What have I done . . . that I should meet such a fate?"[50] The Sapa Inca seemed to blame the governor: "And from your hands, too, you who have met with my friendship and kindness from my people, with whom I have shared my treasures, who have received nothing but benefits from my hands!"[51] The Sapa Inca then begged Pizarro to spare his life. He promised to guarantee the safety of every Spaniard in Peru. The doomed man even pledged to double the already paid ransom. But Pizarro could do nothing. The sentence of death could not be canceled. Atahualpa was going to die. Witnesses claim that he then realized his fate and faced it bravely.

Trumpets sounded to mark the beginning of the execution ceremony. Two hours after sunset, guards led Atahualpa into the great square of Cajamarca. His hands and feet were chained. Torches lit up the night. As he was led to the place of execution, Father Valverde went with him. To the end, the Catholic priest tried to persuade the Incan leader to accept Christianity.

Atahualpa was tied to the stake. Men with torches stood ready to light the brush around the stake. Father Valverde then intervened. He offered a

After he was found guilty of treason, Atahualpa was executed by garroting, which is to slowly choke someone to death. By adopting Christianity, Atahualpa avoided being burned at the stake.

compromise to the former ruler: If Atahualpa adopted Christianity, he would not be burned at the stake. The captive Inca quickly agreed to avoid being burned. Thus, just before his execution, Atahualpa was baptized. Father Valverde gave him the Christian name of Juan (de Atahualpa). Juan is Spanish for John. Atahualpa begged Pizarro to look after his young children. The Sapa Inca also asked that his body be returned to Quito for burial with his ancestors. Then, while several Spanish onlookers prayed aloud for his soul, they killed Atahualpa by garroting him. This means that they placed a thick rope around his neck and slowly choked him to death.

After his execution, with full Christian ceremony and rites, the Spanish buried Atahualpa's body in the Church of San Francisco in Cajamarca. It did not stay there for long. It is believed that some of Atahualpa's followers later dug up the remains. Most likely, they carried his body to Quito for burial in accordance with Incan customs.

De Soto, Atahualpa's friend, returned a few days later, having found no evidence of any Incan army in the surrounding countryside. The execution of Atahualpa in his absence greatly angered de Soto. The emperor's friend rightly believed that Pizarro and the others had deceived him. Hernando de Soto confronted the governor, but the aging conquistador blamed Father Valverde and the others for Atahualpa's death. De Soto argued that he could have taken Atahualpa to Spain to stand trial before King Charles. For de Soto, it was all in vain. His friend, the emperor of the Incan Empire—Atahualpa—was dead.

FIGHTING FOR CONTROL

At first, the death of Atahualpa did little except make it harder for Pizarro to control the Inca. The conquistador replaced Atahualpa with a puppet

Later Adventures of De Soto

Hernando de Soto played a key role in Pizarro's conquest of the Incas. He brought much needed troops and horses with him when he joined the 1531–1534 expedition. De Soto acted as a scout and envoy for Pizarro. The first Spaniard to meet Atahualpa, de Soto opposed any talk of executing the Inca emperor. Despite their friendship, Pizarro succeeded in putting Atahualpa to death.

After his exploits in Peru, de Soto gained lasting fame for leading an expedition that explored the Southeast United States (1539–1542) while searching for gold. On this journey, de Soto and his men became the first Europeans to cross the Appalachian Mountains. Historians also credit the group with discovering the Mississippi River. It was a mammoth journey, traveling more than 4,000 miles. All the while, members of the expedition kept detailed notes of the lands and people they saw.

ruler, named Tupac Huallca. To exercise greater control, Pizarro decided to capture Cuzco. As he made his way toward the capital city, Tupac Huallpa died. Worse still for Pizarro were the loyal followers

> After reaching the Mississippi River, de Soto headed south to see if the river flowed into the Gulf of Mexico. While on this expedition, de Soto became sick with a fever. He died on May 21, 1542. To keep his death secret from the local Indians, his men weighted his body down and placed it in the Mississippi River.
>
> Hernando de Soto and his men never found rich cities or large stores of gold. Instead, the former comrade of Pizarro's died a "disappointed, disillusioned, and financially ruined man."[*] Despite this view, his expedition revealed a vast land, rich in potential for growing crops. De Soto and his men did not realize that the lands they explored would later become part of the United States.
>
> [*] Richard E. Bohlander (editor), *World Explorers and Discoverers* (New York: Da Capo Press, 1998), 405.

of Atahualpa. They attacked the Spaniards in a series of raids, but were mostly unsuccessful.

But Pizarro also found allies from among the Indian tribes. Like Cortés in Mexico, the Spanish conqueror found aid from those who hated the Inca rulers. Two tribes that had suffered under Inca rule, the Cañari and Huanca, hailed the Spanish as liberators. The Spanish, however, simply replaced the Inca as their rulers.

Pizarro still faced resistance from the Inca population. As he pondered the situation, a younger brother of Huáscar's came to him. The brother was Manco, who had somehow managed to escape Atahualpa's supporters. Manco asked Pizarro for help in claiming the Inca throne. Since Pizarro was about to enter Cuzco, a deal was struck between the two. The two became allies as they fought against the forces loyal to the now-dead Atahualpa.

THE INCA REVOLT

Once Pizarro had conquered the Inca, he began ruling Peru. In January 1535, he built his capital city near the coast, within sight of the Pacific Ocean. The city was on the Rimac River, which furnished fresh water from the Andes Mountains. Pizarro named his capital *El Ciudad de los Reyes*, which means, *the City of the Kings*. The city quickly became one of the leading Spanish cities in Peru. Two years later, the Spanish established the port of Callao to help meet the shipping and commerce needs of the capital. Today, *El Ciudad de los Reyes* is called Lima and still serves as the capital of Peru.

Back in Cuzco, Manco ruled under the watchful eye of Gonzalo and Juan Pizarro. The Pizarro brothers commanded about 100 men. The Spaniards were strong enough to do as they pleased. They kept on stealing gold and other valuables in the city. They abused Manco for fun. They even took his favorite wife from him, abusing her. Manco was humiliated and ready to rid himself and his people of the Spaniards. In October 1535, Manco tried to escape. After the Pizarro brothers captured Manco, they had him tortured and thrown in prison. He probably would have died there, had Hernando Pizarro not returned from Spain and ordered Manco released.

Manco no longer trusted the Spaniards and decided to escape and lead a rebellion. This time, he

The English caricaturist James Gillray drew a work entitled "Pizarro Contemplating Over the Product of His New Peruvian Mine." After conquering the Inca, Pizarro established his capital city near the Pacific coast. That city, Lima, remains the capital of Peru today.

planned more carefully. He sent out a call for an army to assemble and wait for him. Then, in the early spring of 1536, Manco asked for permission to pray at a distant shrine. Manco promised to return with the life-sized idol, made of solid gold. Hernando foolishly agreed and sent only two guards with Manco. The Inca ruler got away from the guards and met up with the army waiting for him at the Valley of Cuzco.

Manco vowed to rid Peru of the Spanish. His armies surrounded Cuzco and Lima. The Spanish in Cuzco suffered greatly. The Spanish defenders faced starvation. Manco and his men burned buildings by setting the thatched roofs on fire. Even though they did not have firearms, the natives used slings to hurl stones as large as baseballs at the Spanish. To offset the advantages of the cavalry, the Inca sacrificed themselves in order to injure the horses. Attacks on the Europeans also came from within the city where the Inca positioned themselves on high walls of buildings. To the Spanish, it seemed as if all of Peru stood against them. But Manco misjudged his strength and decided to wait until all his army arrived before making the final assault on Cuzco.

The Pizarro brothers faced the overwhelming challenge with boldness. Since the Spanish were struggling to maintain their hold on Cuzco, they decided to go on the offensive. The Inca held a strongly fortified fort called Sacsahuaman. The fort was made of stone and included three separate walls of protection. The fort was more like a castle. Always preferring glory to safety, the Pizarro brothers left Cuzco and attacked the heavily defended stronghold of Sacsahuaman. Juan Pizarro led the charge of some 50 cavalry soldiers against the defenders on and behind the stone walls. The attack failed. During the attack, Juan Pizarro was struck in the head by a rock. The injury was serious, and he died later that night.

Despite the death of his brother, Hernando Pizarro renewed the attack the next day. This time, the Spaniards treated the fort like a castle. They made high ladders to climb over the walls of the fort. This time, the Spanish managed to defeat the Inca and capture their fort.

The boldness of the Spanish and the Pizarros paid off. After Sacsahuaman fell, Manco had a difficult time keeping his men together. Many of his fighters were simple farmers who needed to return to their fields. Also, an army led by Francisco Pizarro beat Manco's army outside Lima. Spanish reinforcements began arriving to help put down the revolt. Manco watched helplessly as his army surrounding Cuzco grew smaller each passing day. Finally, even Almagro returned from Chile to help Pizarro in April 1537. Manco lifted the siege and fled to the hills. The last chance at Incan independence fell short.

Test Your Knowledge

1 With what crime was Emperor Atahualpa charged?

  a. Polygamy

  b. Promoting idolatry

  c. Making an illegal claim to the Incan throne

  d. All of the above

2 How was Atahualpa executed?

  a. He was beheaded.

  b. He was burned at the stake.

  c. He was strangled with a rope.

  d. None of the above.

3 What did Atahualpa agree to do just before his execution?

  a. Convert to Christianity

  b. Give all his gold to the Spaniards

  c. Put a curse on the Spaniards and their descendants

  d. None of the above

4 How did the Spaniards treat Manco?

  a. The Spaniards revered Manco as a great spiritual leader.

  b. The Spaniards taunted, tortured, and jailed Manco.

  c. The Spaniards forged a treaty with Manco that would last for centuries.

  d. None of the above.

5 Which of the following doomed the Incan revolt?

a. Spanish reinforcements and superior weapons eventually wore down the rebellion.

b. The Spaniards received help from the French in putting down the rebellion.

c. An outbreak of smallpox greatly reduced the number of Incan warriors.

d. None of the above.

ANSWERS: 1. d; 2. c; 3. a; 4. b; 5. a

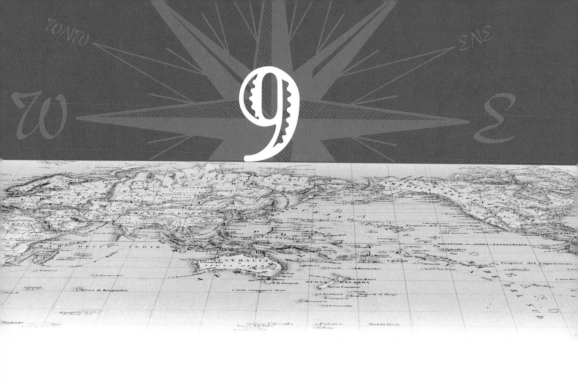

The End
of Pizarro

THE RETURN OF ALMAGRO

The threat of the Incan rebels was over, but Pizarro now faced a more capable foe: his old enemy, Almagro. In 1534, the king of Spain appointed Diego de Almagro governor of Chile (then called New Toledo), located south of Peru. The next year, Almagro and his men proceeded to Chile to acquire gold and silver, just as Pizarro had done in Peru. Unfortunately, Chile was not rich in gold and silver. Almagro felt cheated. Soon, Almagro returned north. At first, Pizarro was thankful that his old friend arrived. Manco had surrounded Cuzco. Almagro and his men were returning from Chile when they received word of the revolt. They swiftly returned to Cuzco to fight Manco. Almagro and his army met Manco's forces in battle, defeating them. All seemed well, but trouble soon followed. As soon as Almagro and his forces entered Cuzco, they arrested the Spaniards there—Spaniards loyal to Pizarro.

Almagro still believed that the aging conquistador had cheated him out of land and wealth. The center of the conflict focused on the city of Cuzco. Almagro and the Pizarro brothers disagreed over who was supposed to rule the city. Since he had won the battle against Manco, Almagro believed the city fell under his control. Meanwhile, the Pizarro brothers all claimed it belonged to them.

To end the dispute, Francisco Pizarro sent an army from Lima to free those Spaniards held by Almagro. Pizarro's brother Hernando commanded this army. But in July 1537, Almagro defeated that army. He also captured Hernando. Next, Almagro decided to attack Pizarro's capital city of Lima. He hoped to rule Peru alone.

Francisco Pizarro realized the danger. As he often had in the past, Pizarro acted with boldness. And he did so quickly and deceitfully. First, he arranged a meeting with his former partner. The two met in November to discuss the situation. Since Cuzco was the main point of the disagreement, the two agreed to let the king of Spain decide the issue. As part of the deal, Almagro let Francisco's brother Hernando go free. Soon after his release, Hernando Pizarro began raising an army to attack Almagro.

Hernando and Almagro met in battle on April 25, 1538. The battle took place outside Cuzco at Las Salinas. Almagro and his men fought fiercely, but in the end the forces commanded by Hernando Pizarro won the battle. This time, Hernando captured Almagro and placed him in prison. Then, Hernando charged him with treason for rebelling against his brother Francisco.

Almagro begged for his life, reminding Hernando of his earlier kindness when he released the younger

Diego de Almagro was executed in 1538 under orders from Pizarro's brother, Hernando. Almagro believed Francisco Pizarro cheated him out of land and wealth. He and the Pizarro brothers had fought over who was to rule the city of Cuzco.

Pizarro from his custody. Despite Almagro's pleas, Hernando showed him no mercy. Pizarro's former friend and partner, Diego de Almagro, was beheaded on July 8, 1538. It appeared that no one stood in opposition to Francisco Pizarro as he controlled all of Peru. But the end of Pizarro's control in Peru was coming.

DEATH CONQUERS THE CONQUEROR

Unfortunately, Almagro's death did not end the hostility. Instead, Almagro's supporters, led by a friend of Almagro's, continued to hate Pizarro. They plotted against the ruler, waiting for the right opportunity to strike him down. Finally, on Sunday, June 26, 1541, they struck. The plan depended upon Pizarro leaving his palace to attend church at the cathedral in Lima. Pizarro learned of the plot, but did not believe it. He decided, however, to take no chances, and stayed home that day. Almagro's supporters realized their chance was slipping away. They altered their plans. Instead of waiting another week, they acted quickly.

While Pizarro and some friends were eating, a group of armed men forced their way into his home. Although several fought bravely to protect Pizarro—now in his late 60s—the Almagro forces were too strong. Pizarro ordered the doors to his private quarters barred, but some of his servants and friends instead tried in vain to fight off the attackers. The attackers soon overwhelmed the mostly unarmed men and made their way deeper into the house.

While several of Pizarro's servants and friends fought to the death, the aging conquistador tried to put on his armor. Lacking the time, he bravely fought against the large group of attackers. Pizarro killed two with his sword before one of the attackers struck him. He fell to the floor, bleeding. Lying on the floor, he drew a cross on the floor with his own blood. As he leaned forward to kiss the cross, another blow from one of the assassins ended his life. A violent death came to the violent conqueror.

After killing Pizarro, the band of murderous thugs declared Almagro's son, also named Diego, the governor of Peru. But the Spanish government was not pleased with the unrest and violence in the colony. An official of the king arrived soon after Pizarro's death. The king authorized him to look into Peru's conditions and make a report to Spain. The king also instructed his official to become the governor if anything had happened to Pizarro. The royal official quickly raised an army to put down the rebellion. The new governor captured the young Almagro after defeating him in battle. Later, the new governor of Peru executed him.

PIZARRO'S BROTHERS

Pizarro's half-brothers all met ignoble ends. Juan Pizarro, of course, died in 1536 from wounds he received in the battle against Manco. Hernando Pizarro returned to Spain to make a report to the king on behalf of Francisco. Word of his role in Almagro's death reached Europe before he did.

Pizarro's Children

Francisco Pizarro had four children by three women. One son and his mother, whose names are not known, died in 1544. Pizarro had two children, a son and a daughter, with an Indian named Inés Huaillas Yupanqui. The son from this union was named for Pizarro's father, Gonzalo, and the daughter, Francisca. Pizarro successfully went through the legal process of having both children declared legitimate in 1537, but Gonzalo died at age 14. Francisca later married, but little else is known about her. Pizarro's fourth child, a son named Francisco, was born to a female relative of Atahualpa's. The child was never legitimized and died shortly after arriving in Spain.

Charles placed Hernando in prison, and he was held there for 20 years. Gonzalo Pizarro, another of Francisco's half-brothers, later led a rebellion for Peru's independence from Spain. At first, the movement was successful. While he ruled Peru, war continued against the Incas, led by Manco. In 1544, Manco was killed, ending the last real threat to Spanish rule in Peru. Eventually the Spanish government raised an army that defeated and captured Gonzalo. In 1548, Spanish authorities executed him.

PERU AFTER PIZARRO

Pizarro's conquest of the Inca forever changed his home country of Spain. The Inca Empire, now called Peru, became an important part of the Spanish Empire. Inca gold filled the Spanish treasury, making Spain one of the wealthiest European countries. Inca gold also helped Spain become a powerful nation. All this wealth from Peru helped Spain become one of the leading European nations throughout the 1500s.

The Spanish conquest also changed Peru and much of South America. After Spain brought Peru

CAPITAN GENERAL
DON FRANCISCO PIZARRO

The mummified remains of Francisco Pizarro are encased in a tomb in Lima Cathedral. Supporters of Almagro's son assassinated Pizarro in 1541.

into its empire, other explorers set out from Peru to conquer other parts of the continent. Explorers from Pizarro's Peru founded both Chile (south of Peru) and Ecuador (north of Peru). Much like Pizarro and Father Luque had dreamed, many of the people in the region converted to Catholicism. Besides Christianity, the Spanish also brought other cultural traits. The Spanish language became the most common language in South America. It still is today.

Francisco Pizarro, the brutal conqueror and destroyer of the Incan culture, suffered a brutal death. His body was buried in a corner of the cathedral in Lima. His mummified remains may still be seen there today.

Test Your Knowledge

1 Why did Diego de Almagro resent Pizarro?
   a. He felt that Pizarro had deserted him in battle against the Incas.
   b. He felt that Pizarro had cheated him out of gold, silver, and land.
   c. He felt that Pizarro had made an illegal alliance with the Incas.
   d. None of the above.

2 How was Diego de Almagro executed?
   a. He was burned at the stake.
   b. He was strangled with a rope.
   c. He was beheaded.
   d. He was shot by a firing squad.

3 In the end, Pizarro was killed by
   a. malaria.
   b. smallpox.
   c. Inca warriors still loyal to Atahualpa.
   d. Spaniards loyal to Almagro.

4 What became of Pizarro's brother Hernando?
   a. He was killed in battle with the Incas.
   b. He returned to Spain and was jailed for 20 years.
   c. He was executed by the Spanish for leading a revolt.
   d. None of the above.

5 Where is the body of Francisco Pizarro today?
   a. Peru
   b. Spain
   c. Chile
   d. None of the above

ANSWERS: 1. b; 2. c; 3. d; 4. b; 5. a

1475(?) Francisco Pizarro is born in Trujillo, Spain.

1502   Pizarro journeys to the West Indies.

1509   Pizarro goes with Alonzo de Ojeda on an expedition to northern Colombia (the Gulf of Uraba).

1513   Pizarro serves as captain on the Darien expedition, in which Vasco Núñez de Balboa discovers the Pacific Ocean.

1521   Hernándo Cortés conquers the Aztec Empire.

1524   Pizarro sails along the Pacific coast of South America for the first time.

1475 (?) Francisco Pizarro is born in Trujillo, Spain.

1502 Pizarro journeys to the West Indies.

1532 Pizarro captures the ruler of the Incas, Atahualpa, on November 16.

1475

1513 Pizarro serves as captain on the Darien expedition, in which Vasco Núñez de Balboa discovers the Pacific Ocean.

1529 Pizarro gains permission to conquer Peru from the king of Spain.

1525–27 A smallpox epidemic strikes Peru.

1526 Pizarro, Diego de Almagro, and Hernando de Luque agree to divide the spoils of their expedition into Peru.

1526–27 Pizarro sails along the Pacific coast a second time; draws a line in the sand when ordered to return to Panama.

1529 Pizarro gains permission to conquer Peru from the king of Spain.

1532 Pizarro captures the ruler of the Incas, Atahualpa, on November 16.

1533 Pizarro executes Atahualpa on August 29.

1538 Pizarro allows his brother Hernando to execute Diego de Almagro.

1541

1535 Pizarro founds Lima, Peru, on January 6.

1541 Followers of Almagro's son murder Francisco Pizarro on June 26 in Lima.

1533 Pizarro executes Atahualpa on August 29.

1533 Pizarro crowns Manco as the Sapa Inca.

1535 Pizarro founds Lima, Peru, on January 6.

1536–37 The Inca revolt against Spanish rule, but are eventually put down.

1538 Pizarro allows his brother Hernando to execute Almagro.

1541 Followers of Almagro's son murder Francisco Pizarro on June 26 in Lima.

Chapter 1
An Important Choice

1. Philip Ainsworth Means, *Fall of the Inca Empire and the Spanish Rule in Peru: 1530–1780* (New York: Gordian Press Inc., 1964), 31.
2. Cecil Howard, *Pizarro and the Conquest of Peru* (New York: American Heritage Publishing Co. Inc., 1968), 71.
3. Ibid.
4. Ibid.

Chapter 2
Pizarro and His World

5. William H. Prescott, *History of the Conquest of Peru: With a Preliminary View of the Civilization of the Incas* (New York: A.L. Burt Company, n.d.), 160.
6. Ibid.
7. Ibid.

Chapter 3
Spain in the New World

8. Alan Lloyd, *The Spanish Centuries* (New York: Doubleday, 1968), 73.
9. Ibid.
10. Morison, Samuel Eliot, *The European Discovery of America: The Southern Voyages, A.D. 1492–1616.* (New York: Oxford University Press, 1974), 77.
11. Lloyd, *The Spanish Centuries,* 73.

Chapter 5
More Failures

12. Prescott, *History of the Conquest of Peru,* 164.
13. Howard, *Pizarro and the Conquest of Peru,* 18.
14. Ibid., 18, 20.
15. Ibid., 55.
16. Ibid.
17. William H. Prescott, *History of the Conquest of Mexico and History of the Conquest of Peru* (New York: Random House, 1989), 878–879.
18. Prescott, *History of the Conquest of Peru,* 229.
19. Ibid.

Chapter 6
The Inca Before Pizarro's Conquest

20. Michael A. Malpass, *Daily Life in the Inca Empire* (Westport, CT: Greenwood Press, 1996), 65.
21. Ibid.
22. Ibid.
23. Ibid.
24. Ibid.
25. Means, *Fall of the Inca Empire and the Spanish Rule in Peru,* 4.
26. William H. Prescott, *The World of Incas* (Geneva: Minerva, A Pierre Waleffe Book, 1970), 19.
27. Ibid, 19.
28. Ibid, 19.
29. Malpass, *Daily Life in the Inca Empire,* 101.
30. Ibid.

31. Ibid.
32. Means, *Fall of the Inca Empire and the Spanish Rule in Peru,* 4.
33. Ibid.
34. Ibid., 3.
35. Garcilaso de la Vega, *The Incas* (New York: Avon Books, 1961), 343.
36. Ibid.
37. Ibid.
38. Ibid.

Chapter 7
The Conquest of Peru

39. John Hemming. *The Conquest of the Incas* (New York: Harcourt Brace Jovanovich, Inc., 1970), 32.
40. Ibid.
41. Ibid.

42. Ibid., 33
43. Prescott, *History of the Conquest of Peru,* 298.
44. Ibid.
45. Ibid., 303.
46. Hemming, *The Conquest of the Incas,* 43.
47. Prescott, *History of the Conquest of Peru,* 308.
48. Hemming, *The Conquest of the Incas,* 45.
49. Prescott, *History of the Conquest of Peru,* 316.

Chapter 8
Pizarro Struggles to Keep Control

50. Prescott, *History of the Conquest of Mexico and History of the Conquest of Peru,* 974.
51. Ibid.

Bohlander, Richard E. (editor). *World Explorers and Discoverers.* New York: Da Capo Press, 1998.

Bowen, J. David. *The Land and People of Peru.* Philadelphia and New York: J.B. Lippincott Company, 1963.

Diamond, Jared. "The Arrow of Disease," *Discover*, October 1992.

Hemming, John. *The Conquest of the Incas.* New York: Harcourt Brace Jovanovich Inc., 1970.

Howard, Cecil. *Pizarro and the Conquest of Peru.* New York: American Heritage Publishing Co. Inc., 1968.

Lloyd, Alan. *The Spanish Centuries.* New York: Doubleday, 1968.

Malpass, Michael A. *Daily Life in the Inca Empire.* Westport, CT: Greenwood Press, 1996.

Means, Philip Ainsworth. *Fall of the Inca Empire and the Spanish Rule in Peru: 1530–1780.* New York: Gordian Press Inc., 1964.

Morison, Samuel Eliot, *The European Discovery of America: The Southern Voyages, A.D. 1492–1616.* New York: Oxford University Press, 1974.

Moseley, Michael E. *The Incas and Their Ancestors.* London: Thames & Hudson Inc., 1992 & 2002.

Prescott, William H. *History of the Conquest of Mexico and History of the Conquest of Peru.* New York: Random House, 1989.

Prescott, William H. *History of the Conquest of Peru: With a Preliminary View of the Civilization of the Incas.* New York: A.L. Burt Company, n.d.

Prescott, William H. *The World of the Incas.* Geneva: Minerva (A Pierre Waleffe Book), 1970.

Vega, Garcilaso de la. *The Incas.* New York: Avon Books, 1961.

Books

Ingram, Scott. *Francisco Pizarro.* San Diego: Blackbirch Press, 2002.

Jacobs, William Jay. *Pizarro: Conqueror of Peru.* New York: Franklin Watts, 1994.

Kachurek, Sandra J. *Francisco Pizarro: Explorer of South America.* Berkeley Heights, NJ: Enslow Publishers Inc., 2004.

Manning, Ruth. *Francisco Pizarro.* Chicago: Heinemann Library, 2001.

Ramen, Fred. *Francisco Pizarro: The Exploration of Peru and the Conquest of the Inca.* New York: The Rosen Publishing Group Inc., 2004

Worth, Richard. *Pizarro and the Conquest of the Incan Empire in World History.* Berkeley Heights, NJ: Enslow Publishers, Inc., 2000.

Websites

Conquistadors: The Conquest of the Incas
http://www.pbs.org/conquistadors/pizarro/pizarro_flat.html

The Conquest of the Inca Empire: Francisco Pizarro
http://www.acs.ucalgary.ca/applied_history/tutor/eurvoya/inca.html

Francisco Pizarro
http://www.famousamericans.net/franciscopizarro

Dr. Shane Mountjoy is an associate professor of history at York College, in York, Nebraska. There he resides with his wife, Vivian, and the two home-school their four daughters. Professor Mountjoy teaches history, geography, and political science courses. He earned an associate of arts degree from York College, a bachelor of arts degree from Lubbock Christian University, a master of arts from the University of Nebraska-Lincoln, and a doctor of philosophy from the University of Missouri-Columbia. He has taught since 1990.

William H. Goetzmann is the Jack S. Blanton, Sr. Chair in History and American Studies at the University of Texas, Austin. Dr. Goetzmann was awarded the Joseph Pulitzer and Francis Parkman Prizes for American History, 1967, for *Exploration and Empire: The Explorer and the Scientist in the Winning of the American West.* In 1999, he was elected a member of the American Philosophical Society, founded by Benjamin Franklin in 1743, to honor achievement in the sciences and humanities.